D0307033

Rainer Zinngrebe

Executive Chef, The Fullerton Hotel

beyond fusion

A new look at ethnic influences on contemporary cooking

Photography by SC Shekar

FLAME
OF THE
FOREST

First published by
Flame Of The Forest Publishing Pte Ltd
Blk 5 Ang Mo Kio Industrial Pk 2A
#07-22/23 AMK Tech II
Singapore 567760
Tel 65-484 8887
Email mail@flameoftheforest.com
www.flameoftheforest.com

Copyright © Flame Of The Forest Publishing, 2001

Photography
SC Shekar

Design
Chimera Design Sdn Bhd
www.chimera.com.my

Editor
Julie Massey

Printed by
Craft Print International Ltd, Singapore

All rights reserved. No part of this
publication may be reproduced or
transmitted in any form or by any
means, electronic or mechanical,
photocopy, recording, or any
information storage system, without
written permission from the Publisher.

ISBN 981-3056-45-2

NORTH TYNESIDE COLLEGE

LEARNING RESOURCE CENTRE

CLASS No	ACCESSION No
641.5992 ZIN	OS3977

SS-00   10

3 B8/11

641.599 ZIN

For Gill, my wonderful wife. Without her support and understanding, I would not have made it this far. Thanks, Schnuck!

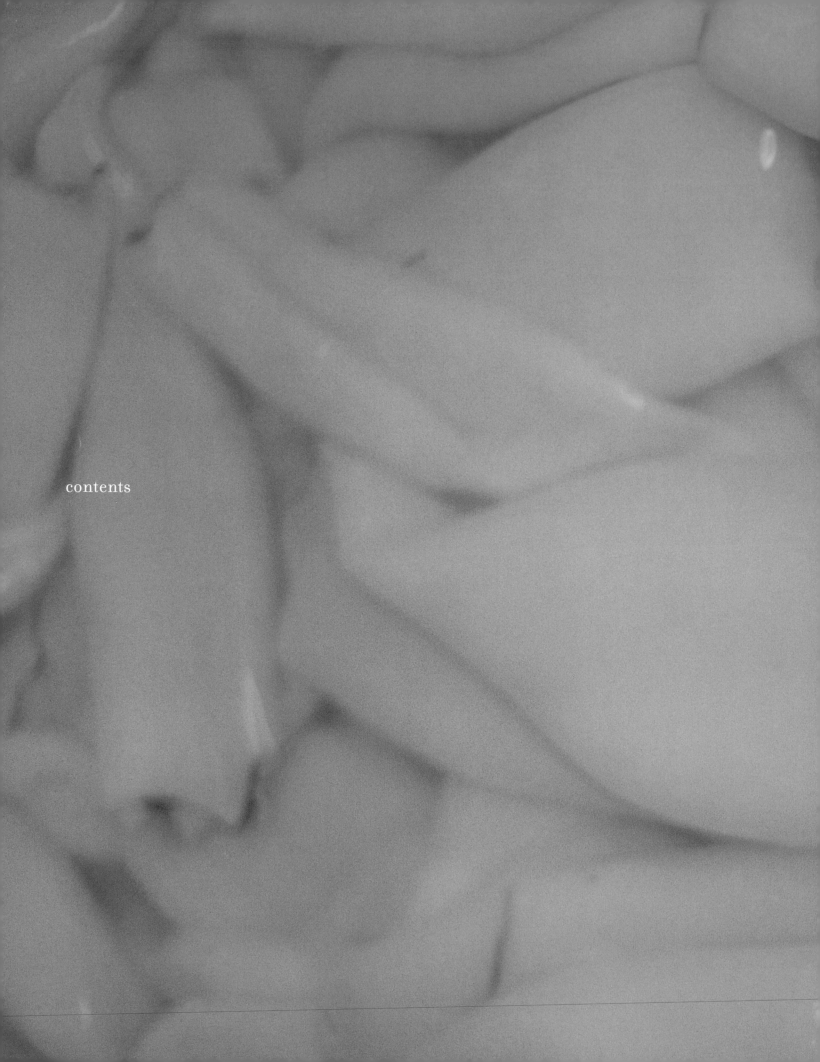

contents

foreword

Anton Mossiman

It gives me infinite pleasure to make people happy with good food and I recognise that same passion in Rainer.

The joy of travelling is that one is constantly exposed to a wealth of fresh ideas, new ingredients, different cuisines and nowhere more so than in the Far East. I have been lucky to be able to do this, and am delighted to find that Rainer has also managed to capture those elements in his book in a style that is both innovative and exciting.

Fusion, with its rich blend of cooking styles, is a book for today, and will be a valuable addition to your bookshelf.

Happy cooking!

Pierre Koffman
La Tante Claire

Rainer was one of the most brilliant young chefs to graduate from my restaurant La Tante Claire in Chelsea.

I remember his lightness of touch, his skills with knife and his flair and originality. In twenty years he has travelled widely, studying and savouring the cuisine of the world.

In this book, he brings together the intense and sensual tastes of France and combines these with the purity and piquancy of the Orient. He communicates the perfectionism of the professional chef who follows the old adage: "Practice until you never get it wrong."

Heureux qui comme Rainer fait un beau voyage.

f

The Fullerton Singapore
Julie Massey

The Fullerton Building has been a landmark in Singapore since its completion in 1928. This imposing structure, strategically sited at the mouth of the Singapore River, has housed the General Post Office, The Exchange, The Chamber of Commerce and The Singapore Club. It has witnessed history in the making, and remains a sign of Singapore's coming of age as a vital hub of commerce and trading.

Structurally, the building represents the solid dignity of Palladian architecture with its classical columns, imposing porticos and decorations. Designed by London architect Major P.H. Keys with assistant architect Mr F. Dowdeswell, the Fullerton Building reflects the public monument tradition of that time of conveying the might and splendour of the Empire.

In the words of the Governor, Sir Hugh Clifford, it was "a monument worthy of the city". The building dominated the skyline. On its rooftop stood the Lighthouse, which guided ships entering the harbour. It appeared in illustrations and on postcards, and became recognised by travellers all over the world as the symbol of Singapore.

The business community of Singapore has passed through The Fullerton's grand doors. It stands guard over the world's busiest port, and has seen Singapore develop into a leading centre of commerce. The Fullerton Singapore is located in the financial and business district, in close proximity to cultural and entertainment centres.

This historical landmark underwent a transformation to mark the coming of the new Millennium. The Fullerton Singapore, under the watchful eye of expert historians and architects, has become a modern hotel that is the epitome of luxury, efficiency and style. The Fullerton is still dedicated to business, catering for every need of the corporate traveller from high-speed communication to sumptuously comfortable rooms and superb dining. Every meal, whether it is an intimate dinner, power breakfast or company banquet, is guaranteed to be a memorable occasion, thanks to The Fullerton's range of dining choices.

Executive Chef Rainer Zinngrebe was a member of the development team at The Fullerton Hotel prior to the official opening in December 2000. Together with a team of carefully chosen professionals, he created and implemented the varied cuisine styles and high standards vital to a prestigious hotel. The original menus featured established ethnic cuisine, but the discriminating clientele soon showed an interest in cross-cultural dishes. This allowed Chef Rainer and his team to add fusion dishes to the menus.

The restaurants and bars of The Fullerton offer a wide selection of dining styles. The Courtyard, at lobby level, is a relaxing haven where you can enjoy coffee, pastries and sandwiches, traditional afternoon tea, or cocktails in the evening. Jade offers fine Cantonese cuisine in an elegant setting. Award-winning master chefs, using only the best and freshest ingredients, prepare classical and contemporary dishes.

The original Fullerton Lighthouse has become a stunning fine-dining restaurant, offering panoramic views of Marina Bay. Town, a sophisticated restaurant and bar, features several of the recipes in this book on its menu. From its contemporary interior finished in teak and leather to its waterside terrace, it is the perfect place for a relaxing meal, anytime of the day or night. The Post Bar is the hotel's concept bar. Its brilliant contemporary design features the original ceiling of the General Post Office.

the inspiration

A walk in the wet markets and provision stores of Asia — the ultimate culinary adventure.

Joseph Lam

Blame it on the airlines, pruning the distance between the east and west. Blame it on the economic and political wars that make migrants out of all us. Blame it on the rapid globalisation of markets for breaking down the trade barriers. Whatever the reason may be, the result is still the same. The inevitable fusion of cultures has led to a greater availability of food choices around us, and it cannot be denied that this has strongly influenced the direction of contemporary cooking today.

Everyday, more and more Asian produce find its way to the shelves and bins of the Tesco's, Sainsbury's, Zabar's and Balducci's of the West, intriguing western chefs and surprising jaded palates in the process. But inspiring though these food emporia may be, the truth is, for pure, unadulterated inspiration, nothing beats a walk in an Asian wet market. This is the ultimate culinary adventure, the one true Mecca for the fervent foodie.

However, the typical Asian wet market is not for the faint-hearted. Indeed, it would be an understatement to say that it is a full-on assault on your senses – and an open snub in the face of the pristine orderliness and sterility of the modern supermarket. Teeming with throngs of people jostling you every which way you turn, it is at once noisy, odorous and mesmerizing.

Around you, a cacophony of voices cry out their prices in singsong rhymes, speaking in different languages, and scores of inpenetrable dialects and accents, bargaining, haggling, complaining, and sharing tips. Before you, the myriad choices of fresh vegetables, fruits, fish and meat on display make up a dazzling kaleidoscope of brilliant colours and unfamiliar shapes. The floor sloshes and squelches underfoot, from being kept perpetually wet and slippery as the traders liberally water their vegetables and replenish the ice that keep their fish fresh – and you begin to understand why it is called a wet market. Then there are the smells – fresh, perfumed and familiar yet at the same time different, fetid even, every scent made more pungently potent as it melds with the humid air and increasing temperatures, creating a heady cocktail for those of a delicate constitution.

This is the temple to which the majority of Asian housewives make their daily pilgrimage for fresh food, household wares and other necessities. This is the source that fuels and inspires Asia's phenomenally varied cuisine, and which has catalyzed the fusion food movement around the world. Yet, for all the wonderful treasures it holds, its setting, in cities and large towns alike, is more often than not located in a charmless modern block, so anonymous and claustro-phobic that the average tourist wouldn't even give its discovery a second thought. Its country counterpart, however, in the smaller towns and villages, offers a far more traditional and aesthetically pleasing prospect, drawing the curious visitor or serious culinary devotee on into its exotic, bazaar-like atmosphere, sprawled out across an open square, under a sea of colourful umbrellas to shelter shoppers from the sweltering heat and humidity.

For the uninitiated, the market may seem to be randomly laid out with little logic at times, but there is, in fact, a method to this seeming madness. Much like a supermarket, the traders are organized around the types of goods they sell, and have undoubtedly been so for centuries. The vegetable traders have invariably occupied the largest area in the market, given the

sheer variety of their produce. There is practically nothing that can't be found here; from the familiar staples to the more delightfully exotic – angled loofahs, hairy gourds, drumstick pods, stinky beans, lotus roots – a list as long as your curiosity and patience last. Here, determined housewives, calling for attention, match the traders' hollering, decibel for decibel. Wagging fingers point and prod in search of the most tender Hong Kong Choy Sam, the crispest sweet peas, celery jet-fresh from the Netherlands – nothing less than the finest, blemish-free produce for today's breakfast, lunch, dinner and supper.

Nearby are found the fishmongers, where here again the choice is breathtaking – Star Groupers, Leopard Coral Trouts, Napoleon Wrasses, Bamboo Fish, Barramundis, King Salmons, Tiger Prawns, Mantis Shrimps. Whatever your choice, the fish are sold whole or cut to order, and the scaling, gutting and cleaning are done in a fraction of the time it took you to overcome your indecision. These two sections, often the wettest part of the market, are where the pace is frenetic, unrelenting, and the competition fiercest.

In another section of the market, the panicked cries of the batteries of hens, ducks and geese drown out the poultry sellers' exhortations to customers. As selections are made, the ill-fated animals are immediately slaughtered and unceremoniously thrown into a heaving, metal contraption, to be processed, cleaned and ready to be picked up in 20 minutes or less. A short distance away, portly butchers stand testament to the quality of their goods – with hunks of freshly slaughtered meat hanging on hooks as well as laid out on cement slabs. Wielding huge cleavers, their determined chopping through flesh and bone send grisly echoes throughout the hall. Reflecting the sensitivities of a multicultural society and plurality of religions, Muslim butchers would congregate a discreet distance away from the non-halal (or non-kosher) meat vendors, where they conduct their business and ply their trade; an example of the tolerance and spirit of accommodation found in this colourful amorphous entity.

As you meander your way to drier ground, which could well be on an upper floor, this is where you are likely to encounter the traders in dry provisions. Quieter, cooler, drier, here the mood is visibly relaxed. There's now more time for a smile, for catching up with customers who have become old friends. Walk into any cubicle here, and you enter a palpably different world altogether. The air is redolently pungent with

a hundred mesmerizing fragrances, sometimes choking, at other times soothing, the walls piled high with cans, bottles and jars of pickles, sauces, marinades, vinegars, and oils. Practically every inch of the floor space is made use of, stacked with barrels, bins, crates, gunny sacks, paper bags of rice, lentils, dried chillies and ground spices. Even the ceiling space is utilized, with baskets suspended in midair, laden with packets, sachets, bunches, bundles of prepared pastes, condiments, noodles and such like. The origins of the goods are from as far away as China, Hong Kong, Taiwan and Japan, to countries closer to home, such as the Philippines, Vietnam, Thailand, Malaysia, Indonesia, and even the Indian subcontinent.

Outside, is a motley collection of food hawkers with their pushcarts peddling their foods to the waiting husbands, the impatient children and shoppers emerging to catch their breaths. There are steaming pots of sweet corn freshly boiled in brine, freshly roasted chestnuts in blackened woks, steamed flour

rolls with an assortment of sauces, and a host of other delicacies to choose from. The ice cream seller hovering nearby, does a brisk business under the fierce midday sun.

Without doubt, the Asian wet market experience is one of a kind, and with such inspiration so readily found in its halls, it is easy to understand why the people of South-east Asia are incredibly passionate about their food, to the point of becoming obsessive about freshness, taste, texture, technique and creative possibilities. As Asia's different cultures increasingly insinuate their way into the West, while westerners, in ever greater numbers, discover the diversity of Asia's food emporia, it is inevitable that the ensuing crossover of ingredients, concepts and techniques will continue to revolutionize contemporary western cooking. For traditionalists, it might seem sacrilegious, but for the rest of us, the future of cooking can only look brighter indeed.

the interpretation

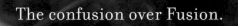

The confusion over Fusion.

Joseph Lam

Fusion-style cooking today exists in many forms and is known by many names. Some people call it called East-West cuisine... others Pan-Asian or Pan-Pacific cuisine, and even Pacific Rim cuisine. At one time or another, we've all played guinea pigs to various ambitious interpretations of this often misunderstood genre of cooking, and let's be honest, in a lot of cases, we've ended up wondering if Confusion Cooking might have been a better name for it.

Admittedly, it's easy for us to dismiss Fusion-style cooking as a waste of effort and money, but surely this is a bit unfair. There really is no such thing as bad fusion – more often than not, it is more likely to be a case of bad cooking! These terms have often been wrongly bandied about in justification of what is nothing more than a poorly tossed salad of Asian flavours and ingredients, which have been inappropriately matched and added without any clear direction or judicious choice.

Which brings us to the million-dollar question: What exactly is Fusion-style cooking? There are two schools of thought surrounding this much-debated culinary concept. Without meaning to over-intellectualise the subject, the first explanation is that it is a meeting of different cultures, often brought together by mass migration, historical conquests or centuries of trade, and culminating in shared culinary traditions, ingredients and techniques. The result of this culinary crossover is a natural hybrid of the original, with a more slowly evolved substitution, matching and melding of flavours, textures, and consistencies.

The second is perhaps best explained as an unabashed celebration of the diversity of ingredients and ethnic tastes. This approach favours forced hybridisation, which, in the wrong hands, can result in a severely schizophrenic encounter. It is this that has become a genre of contemporary cooking, a period of deliberate cross-cultural borrowing of flavours and ingredients popularised and glamorised by globetrotting chefs. When compared with the former, there are no real rules, save the chef's own expertise in contemporary cooking techniques and his or her personal taste preferences. And because there are no real rules, it is pretty much hit-or-miss most of the time. For this reason, I personally like to call this the 'Jekyll-and-Hyde' approach.

The fact is, that to even call it Fusion is misleading, and, as a concept in cooking, it is an oxymoron. Of course, flavours fuse when cooking. What would we expect them do? Therein lies the ultimate test of the proverbial pudding – the ability of the chef to sublimely meld the different and often divergent flavours, to evoke an ephemeral recollection of the ingredients' original characteristics and yet maintain the ability to surprise and titillate our taste buds, and ultimately, to satisfy our appetite.

This book is essentially Rainer's very personal interpretation of this genre of cooking, the result of his many years spent in Asia, in Thailand, Malaysia and Singapore, and his fascination with and respect for Asian ingredients and foods. His enthusiasm and passion for experimentation resulting from his close observations and personal encounters with the different people he has worked with and befriended is undeniable. It is perhaps these very qualities that separate him from most other proponents of this delicate and subtle style of cooking.

Asia is one big rambunctious market of culinary inspiration waiting to be experienced, its secrets more aptly deciphered and expertly elucidated by people like Rainer. Home to 3.6 billion people, and many surprisingly different cultures and sub-cultures, it should come as

no surprise, therefore, that the average person is exposed daily to myriad varieties of ethnic foods and an even greater number of regional or dialectal variations. Everyday we shamelessly 'borrow' from each other's culinary heritage – and we've been doing that for centuries.

From the time of our early forefathers who traded, laboured, fished and fought their way across the different Asian lands up to the present, our constant exposure to the multifarious cultural culinary traditions has resulted in an instinctive skill for seeking out, adopting and adapting different ethnic tastes to satisfy our gustatory cravings. In Malaysia, in the capital city of Kuala Lumpur alone, a random tour of the everyday food centres that feed its population serves up a mind-boggling choice of over 200 varieties of foods.

It is this fascinating kaleidoscope of choices that fuels our passion for food and our obsession to introduce our taste buds to new heights of culinary genius. Consider for a moment that the average Asian, from

the day he is born and throughout his life, is treated to a culinary feast the likes of which most of the western world will never know. Take breakfast as an instance. For an Asian the concept of an austere meal, of say jam and bread, is beyond comprehension. When he breaks fast, it has to be a celebration of colours, flavours, textures, consistencies and aromas – even with the most basic of foods in the most frugal of homes.

Consider the Nasi Lemak, a morning staple in Malaysia of Malay origin (though hugely popular with Chinese, Indians, Eurasians, and the odd Westerner, alike.) It is nothing more than just rice cooked with coconut milk and thoughtfully scented with the cloyingly sweet fragrance of pandan leaves. It's usually accompanied by the lightly salted flavours of a tablespoon of groundnuts and dried anchovies pan-fried till crispy, a 'heart-warming' sweet and spicy chilli paste or sambal of onion rings cooked till meltingly soft, with a few crisp slices of cucumbers, and one half of a hard boiled egg all neatly wrapped together into a small pyramid with banana leaf which, in turn, lends its

light perfume to the whole package. And that's just the no-frills version.

Consider as well the Roti Canai or Roti Paratha, another favourite breakfast item. It is a flattened Indian bread (made with plain flour, eggs, ghee or clarified butter, fresh or evaporated cow's milk and lightly seasoned with salt and sugar) that is spectacularly kneaded and pulled and punched and spun and folded and pan-fried to a golden crisp pancake. Then, after all this hard work, it is dramatically squashed with the clap of the hands, breaking the crisp pancake into a flurry of paper-thin layers, both crispy and chewy, and served with a saucer of simple, watery fish curry or a creamier lentil and potato curry. Again this is the basic version, but you get the picture.

That we are spoilt for choice in Asia is putting it mildly; for us the absence of variety is unthinkable. Every meal of every day, we struggle hopelessly, comically, with indecision. Is it going to be congee or noodles? Bread or rice? Indian or Chinese? Malaysian,

Indonesian, Filipino, Thai, Burmese or Vietnamese? Or better still, a mix of everything? What all this really boils down to is that it is this very heightened awareness of the choices we have around us that is strongly influencing the direction of contemporary cooking today, whether in Asia or around the world.

In this book, Rainer's refreshing interpretations, though seemingly complex at times, nevertheless manages to surprise often, with his innovative and sometimes irreverent ways with the ingredients every Asian has grown up with. But then, that is the beauty of this book. It is intended to be an inspiration for us, to challenge our preconceptions, to provoke our jaded palates, so that we may boldly taste what we would never have dared taste before. If it persuades even just a handful of people to abandon the fluorescent sterility of the modern supermarket for those twin palaces of a thousand delights – the simply unmatch-able Asian wet market and the ever-humble Asian provision store, then it would have done its job eminently well.

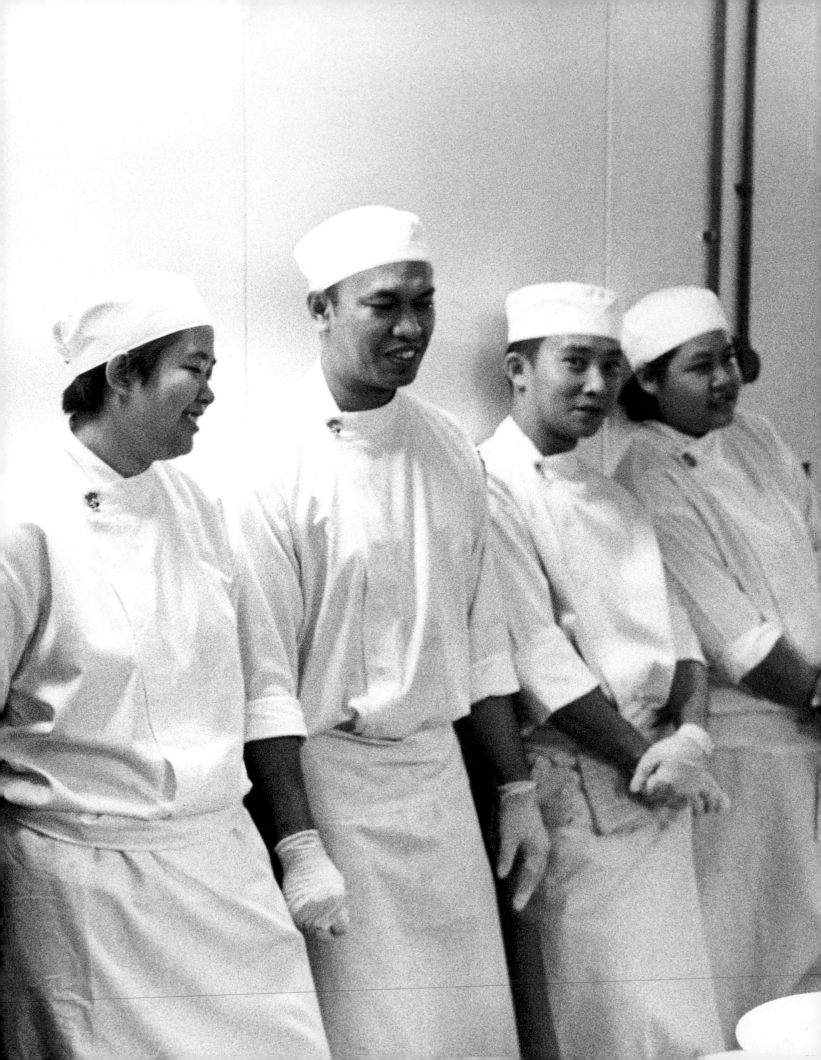

the magic

Soup is my speciality. It is also the perfect medium for fusing flavours. Every culture has its own popular soups, and I have come to appreciate Asian noodle soups for their sense of completeness.

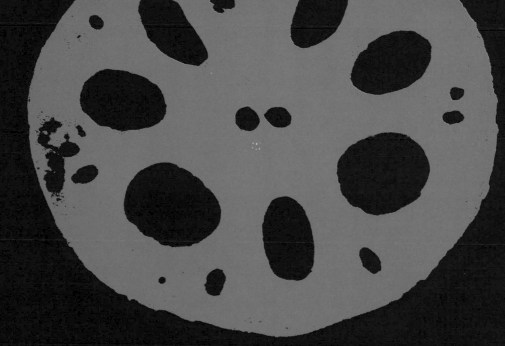

soups and laksa

Black Chicken Herbal Broth

1½ kg (3 lb) whole black chicken

1 kg (2 lb) whole chicken (use an older bird such as a boiling hen)

750 g (1lb 8 oz) chicken feet

500 g (1 lb) smoked turkey off cuts, fried

10 g (1/3 oz – about 1 tsp) dried longan meat (longan yok)

10 g (1/3 oz – about 1 tbsp) red dried dates (hung choe)

25 g (1 oz) yam tuber (wai san)

50 g (2 oz) wolfberries (kei chee)

15 g (½ oz – about 1 tbsp) angelica root (dong kwai)

15 g (½ oz – about 1 tbsp) astragal root (puk chi)

25 g (1 oz) Chilean bellflower (dong sum)

10 g (1/3 oz – about 1 tbsp) rhizome of Solomon's seal (yok chok)

10 g (1/3 oz – about 1 tbsp) star anise

5 litres (10 pints) Asian chicken stock (see Basics Explained)

The herbs' Cantonese names are in brackets. These herbs are available from Chinese medical or herbal shops.

Blanch the chickens quickly in a large pot of boiling water. Skim and strain off all scum and fat, then wash chickens.

Place the chickens, strained blanching water and all other ingredients into a large pot and top up with the stock. Bring to a simmer and cover with lid. Leave to simmer slowly for 6-8 hours.

Remove chicken and herbs – reserve some of the dark chicken meat and herbs for garnish. Strain cooking liquid and reduce to desired concentration.

If served as a soup, add a generous sprinkle of sliced spring onions and a dash of Shao Xing wine.

The Chinese belief in the healing power of herbs stems from their five thousand year old tradition of natural healing. This dish uses not only herbs but also fungi, roots, seeds and other ingredients. The combination of black chicken (a variety with dark grey meat which is said to have medicinal powers) and ingredients like angelica, wolfberries and dried longan meat builds layer upon layer of flavours. This soup makes an excellent base for many dishes.

During my time in Thailand, I particularly enjoyed the local curries. As soup is my speciality, I developed a soup featuring their flavours. When making this soup aim for a balance of tastes, it should not be predominantly spicy or strong.

Thai Red Curry Cappuccino with Honey-Smoked Duck Breast

4 tbsp sunflower oil

1 large onion, sliced

6 tbsp Thai red curry paste
(see Basics Explained)

2 tbsp tomato paste

600 ml (1 pint 3½ fl oz)
coconut cream

4 tbsp palm sugar

1½ litres (3 pints) duck or chicken
stock (see Basics Explained)

3 stalks lemon grass, lightly crushed

1 cup red lentils (use more if you
want thick soup)

5 cm (2 in) piece galangal, sliced

2 kaffir lime leaves

Fish sauce to taste

4 tbsp whipping cream

Slices of honey-smoked duck breast

Heat the oil in a large pot or wok and sauté the onion until transparent. Add the curry paste and sauté for about 5 minutes.

Add the tomato paste and cook for a further 2 minutes. Stir in all the other ingredients and bring to a boil. Reduce heat and leave to simmer for about 45 minutes.

Remove the lemon grass and lime leaves, and then blend the soup until it is smooth. Strain through a fine sieve and bring back to the boil.

Add fish sauce to season and, if needed, more stock. Remove from heat, add whipping cream and froth with a stick blender before serving.

Serve with some thin slices of honey-smoked duck breast, pan-fried on the skin side until almost cooked then turned over to finish off.

As a variation, top with some whipped cream mixed with chopped coriander. This soup could also be served with a deep-fried wan tan filled with Chinese-style roast duck and plum sauce.

Rasam with Seafood

FOR THE RASAM BASE

100ml (3½ fl oz) vegetable oil

2 sprigs curry leaves

4 dried chillies

1 tbsp mustard seeds

1 tbsp cumin seeds, toasted

4 tsp coriander seeds, toasted

2 tsp black peppercorns, toasted

1 bunch coriander roots

10 cloves of garlic, smashed

2½ litres (5 pints) tamarind water
(see Basics Explained)

500 ml (1 pint) water

3 tomatoes

1 carrot, diced

½ cup yellow lentils

FOR SEAFOOD MAIN COURSE

1 small carrot, cut into fine strips

1 small leek, cut into fine strips

4 large tiger prawns, whole

120 g (4 oz) salmon fillet, cubed

120g (4 oz) cod fillet, cubed
(any firm fish can be used)

100 g (3½ oz) fresh crab meat

8 fresh mussels

16 fresh clams

4 fresh scallops

1 tomato, skinned, seeds removed
and cut into fine strips

A few sprigs of fresh coriander

Heat the oil in a large frying pan and sauté the curry leaves, dried chilli and mustard seeds. Next, combine all the other ingredients for the rasam base. Add to the oil mixture and bring to a simmer over medium heat. Reduce heat and simmer for about 1 hour.

Strain the rasam base and add the carrot and leek followed by the seafood, in order according to their cooking times. Simmer over low heat until all the seafood is cooked.

Add the tomato and serve garnished with coriander.

The first time I visited Shekar's house, Peng served this wonderful soup. I was amazed that vegetarian food could be so tasty. Its hot and sour taste is similar to tom yam, so it seemed natural to add seafood. The resulting dish can be served as a seafood course or a fish soup.

This is a favourite dish, exceptionally spicy and full of flavour. Although tom yam has been interpreted in many ways, it refers to a hot and spicy soup only; and to use it (for instance) as 'tom yam sauce' would be wrong. This dish was our winning entry in an Australian Black Box Culinary Challenge in Thailand.

Tom Yam with Sashimi

FOR THE TOM YAM BROTH

200 g (6½ oz) prawn, lobster or yabbie shells

2 litres (4 pints) plain water or a very light fish stock

200 g (6½ oz) tom yam chilli paste (available in most supermarkets)

2 tbsp tomato paste

100 ml (3½ fl oz) peanut oil (corn oil can be substituted)

10 kaffir lime leaves

15 stalks lemon grass, crushed

8 chilli padi (the tiny Asian variety – either green or red. They are extremely hot, use less if desired)

8 stems coriander root

15 cm (6 in) piece galangal root, sliced

5 fresh tomatoes, chopped

Juice of 10 limes

Fish sauce (either Thai or Vietnamese – Nam Pla or Nuoc Nam)

Finely ground white pepper

GARNISH FOR THE SOUP

4 tiger prawns (or more), shelled with tail left on, cooked

100 g (3½ oz) fresh straw mushrooms (the canned variety is fine, cut them in half and drain well)

Small bunch coriander leaves

4 chilli padi

SIDE GARNISH FOR THE SOUP – TO BE SERVED SEPARATELY

4 slices maguro tuna sashimi

4 slices fresh Aquatas salmon sashimi

4 fresh scallops, sliced

4 slices Aquatas lemon-myrtle-smoked salmon

Heat the oil until it smokes in a pot large enough to hold all the ingredients. I use a wok, as the heat distribution is very good.

Fry the cleaned and dried shells over very high heat. Once the shells have turned bright red, turn down the heat to moderate and add the water or stock. Bring to a slow simmer for about 20 minutes, and then add all the other broth ingredients except for the fish sauce, white pepper and lime juice. Remove from heat and set aside to infuse for about 20 minutes.

Strain and simmer over moderate heat, reduce to desired concentration. Add the soup garnish ingredients and season with fish sauce, white pepper and lime juice to taste. Serve with sashimi, scallops and smoked salmon on the side – these can be added to the soup or eaten separately.

Seafood Laksa with Yellow Egg Noodles

FOR THE BROTH

2 tbsp corn oil

450 g (14½ oz) laksa paste
(see Basics Explained)

2 litres (4 pints) fish or chicken stock
(see Basics Explained)

1 bunch Thai basil, stems only

1½ litres (3 pints) coconut milk
(Ayam brand if available)

¼ cup brown sugar

Fish sauce to taste

Juice of 6 limes

FOR THE NOODLES

600 g (1 lb 3½ oz) Chinese yellow
egg noodles

2 litres (4 pints) boiling water

FOR THE SEAFOOD AND
OTHER GARNISH

16 prawns, cooked

16 scallops, cooked

16 red snapper fillets – 30 g (1 oz)
each, cooked

16 sugar snap peas or other
vegetables, cooked

100 g (3½ oz) fresh bean sprouts

FOR THE GARNISH

60 g (2 oz) spring onions, sliced

100 g (3½ oz) fresh shallots, sliced

4 tbsp dry crispy fried shallots

8 limes, cut in half

Heat the oil in a wok over medium heat and add the laksa paste. Fry, stirring constantly for at least 5 minutes or until the paste starts to separate from the oil. This may take up to 10 minutes, depending on the heat source.

Add the stock and bring to a boil, reduce heat and leave to simmer for about 5 minutes, then add the coconut milk and basil stems. Leave to simmer for 20-25 minutes or until sufficiently concentrated.

Strain through a fine sieve and season with the sugar and fish sauce, then add the lime juice. Keep aside until needed.

Bring the water to a boil and blanch the noodles for a few seconds. Remove from water and drain. Reheat the stock, add the seafood and vegetables and heat through.

Place the hot noodles into bowls and top with the stock, seafood and vegetables.

Garnish with spring onion, shallots and bean sprouts. Serve with lime halves on the side.

Not much fusion here, but a delicious introduction to Asian noodle soups. Wet noodle dishes are found throughout Asia, where they are popular as a substantial snack. They can be very light or rather heavy, depending on the stock used. This dish makes a satisfying meal.

During my time in Chicago, I was impressed by American chowder – a thick rich soup containing many ingredients. Over the years, I have revisited these chowders and aimed to stay true to the concept. This is one of my variations.

Roasted Pumpkin and Sweet Corn Chowder with Crispy Fried Crab Meat Wan Tan

FOR THE CHOWER

Small bunch coriander roots

5 cm (2 in) piece ginger, peeled and sliced

1 large medium-hot red chilli, stem removed

3 tbsp vegetable oil

2 stalks lemon grass, smashed

400 g (13 oz) creamed corn kernels

1 litre (2 pints) Asian chicken stock (see Basics Explained)

500 g (1lb) pumpkin, peeled, seeds removed, roasted and mashed

440 ml (14 fl oz) coconut cream

Salt and freshly ground black pepper

FOR THE GARNISH

100 g (3½ oz) pumpkin, cooked and diced

100 g (3½ oz) baby corn, cooked and cut into pieces

4 tbsp plain yoghurt

1 tbsp chopped coriander leaves

8 crab meat wan tans – deep-fried (see Basics Explained)

In a mortar, combine coriander root, chilli and ginger and pound to a paste.

Heat the oil in a large pot or wok and add the paste. Sauté for a few minutes until the flavours are released.

Add the lemon grass and corn kernels. Cook for another minute, and then add the stock, pumpkin and coconut cream. Adjust seasoning with salt and pepper and simmer for about 20 minutes. Puree the soup in a blender until smooth.

Garnish the soup with a generous amount of pumpkin and baby corn. Top with a spoonful of the yoghurt and coriander mixed together.

Serve with crab meat wan tans on the side.

Asian Mushroom Consommé
with Bird's Nest

FOR THE CONSOMMÉ

1200 ml (2 pints 6½ fl oz) litres vegetable stock
(see Basics Explained)

12 dried shiitake mushrooms

15 g (½ oz, about 1 tbsp) dried porcini mushrooms

15 g (½ oz, about 1 tbsp) dried morels

15 g (½ oz, about 1 tbsp) dried chanterelles

30 g (1 oz) dried longan meat *(longan yok)*

50 g (1¾ oz) red dried dates *(hung choe)*

20 g (¾ oz, about 1½ tbsp) angelica root *(dong kwai)*

20 g (¾ oz, about 1½ tbsp) wolfberries *(kei chee)*

20 g (¾ oz, about 1½ tbsp) yam tuber *(wai san)*

20 g (¾ oz, about 1½ tbsp) astragal root *(puk chi)*

FOR THE FINAL SOUP

1 litre (2 pints) consommé

12 cooked dried shiitake mushrooms, sliced

100 g (3½ oz) enoki mushrooms, roots cut off

100 g (3½ oz) shimeji mushrooms, separated
but left whole

100 g (3½ oz) fresh shiitake mushrooms, sliced

200 g (6½ oz) button mushrooms, sliced

8 bird's nests, cleaned (see Basics Explained)

Place all the ingredients for the consommé in a pot
and bring to a boil, then remove from heat and
completely cover the pot with plastic wrap.

Place the pot in a steamer and leave it to steam for
4 - 5 hours; this is a Chinese cooking method called
'double boiling'. Remove from heat and strain.
Add all the final soup ingredients and bring to a
simmer, leave to simmer for about 5 minutes then
check and adjust seasoning.

Chopped chives, Shao Xing wine and some freshly
ground black pepper can be added to serve.

Bird's nest is a traditional Chinese ingredient used in soups and desserts. These swiftlet nests are collected by professional harvesters at great personal risk: the nests are usually found on high cliffs or caves. The best quality nests are very pale in colour, however the most sought after have a slight red tinge. Bird's nest, an expensive delicacy, is also considered a tonic. It has little taste of its own and can be used as an 'added value' ingredient in many dishes.

Laksa is a traditional Malaysian dish made with noodles and thick soupy gravy. Several years of working in Thailand and Malaysia have unmistakably influenced my cooking. My favourite dish in Thailand was Gaeng Kiew Wan Gai (green chicken curry), and one of my favourite Malaysian dishes is Mee Kari Laksa. This recipe is a combination, with the addition of Chinese barbecue chicken to give sweetness to this spicy dish. Udon noodles (Japanese rice flour noodles) supply extra texture. This is a mixture of Thai, Chinese, Japanese and Malaysian with a dominant Thai flavour, a dish I regard as perfect trans-ethnic cuisine.

Green Curry Laksa with Udon Noodles and Chinese Barbecue Chicken

FOR THE CHICKEN

1 kg (2 lb) chicken legs, skin and bones removed

450 g (14½ oz) sugar or honey

160 ml (5 fl oz) light soya sauce

200 g (6½ oz) garlic, very finely minced

1 tsp five spice powder

1 tsp finely ground white pepper

100 ml (3½ fl oz) oyster sauce

1 tbsp brown bean paste

1 tbsp hoi sin sauce

A few drops red food colouring

FOR THE GREEN CURRY

2 tbsp sunflower oil

2 stalks lemon grass, crushed

5 kaffir lime leaves

1 medium onion, sliced

Large piece galangal, sliced

4 tbsp Thai green curry paste

2 tbsp brown sugar

2 tablespoons coriander leaves

1 litre (2 pints) Asian chicken stock (see Basics Explained)

500 ml (1 pint) coconut cream

400 g (14 oz) frozen udon noodles

First prepare the chicken. Combine all the ingredients except the chicken and bring to a boil. Remove from heat and leave to cool down. Pour the cooled mixture over the chicken and leave to marinate for 24 hours in the refrigerator.

Place chicken pieces directly onto a rack with drip pan underneath and roast in a preheated oven at 200°C (390°F). (Traditionally the chicken pieces are hung from a hook in the oven.) This will take about 15 minutes, depending on the thickness of the chicken. Chop into small pieces just before serving.

To make the soup, heat the oil in a large pot or wok over moderate heat. Sauté the lemon grass, kaffir lime leaves, onion and galangal until the onion is transparent. Add the curry paste and fry for another 2-3 minutes to release flavours. Add the sugar, coriander, stock and coconut cream and heat through.

Simmer the noodles for 2-3 minutes in boiling water. Remove from water and drain. To serve, place noodles and green curry soup in serving bowls. Top with barbecue chicken pieces.

Spicy Coconut, Crab and Lemon Grass Bisque

4 tbsp olive oil

1 kg (2 lb) crab shells, or spider crab, cut into walnut-sized pieces

2 medium onions, sliced

2 cloves garlic

2 carrots, chopped

1 stalk celery

1 small leek, chopped – white part only

100 ml (3½ fl oz) brandy or sanghtip (Thai brandy)

2 medium-size pieces galangal, peeled and sliced

4 stalks lemon grass, lightly crushed

3 litres (6 pints) chicken stock

3 tomatoes, baked at 180°C (355°F) for 15 minutes

4 chilli padi, seeds removed and chopped

6 kaffir lime leaves

½ bunch coriander, root and leaves

1 tbsp coriander seeds

440 ml (14 fl oz) coconut cream

Salt and pepper

Heat the olive oil to smoking point in a pot or braising pan that is large enough to hold all the ingredients.

Add the crab and roast over very high heat until all the shells are evenly coloured. Add the onions, garlic, carrot, and celery and roast until they start to brown. Add the other ingredients, except for the coconut cream, and bring to a rapid boil. Reduce heat and leave to simmer for about 25 minutes.

Strain and bring back to a simmer, reduce by a third and then add the coconut cream.

Simmer to reduce to required concentration. Adjust seasoning with salt and pepper just before serving.

Crab (or lobster) bisque is possibly the most popular Western-style soup in Asia. This dish is essentially a 'crab bisque', but by using and adding local ingredients we have turned it into something distinctly Asian. Serve it as a soup, or reduce and use as a laksa stock.

Vegetables are not something
we eat in large quantities in the
Western world. We have staples like
potatoes, carrots and cabbage,
but they are usually side dishes with
limited importance. When I came
to Asia my outlook on vegetables
changed. The abundance all year
round of different vegetables,
the way they are used as main
ingredients and their importance
within a meal made me appreciate
their versatility. Because of friends
like Shekar, I learned that
vegetarian food could be excellent
if properly prepared.

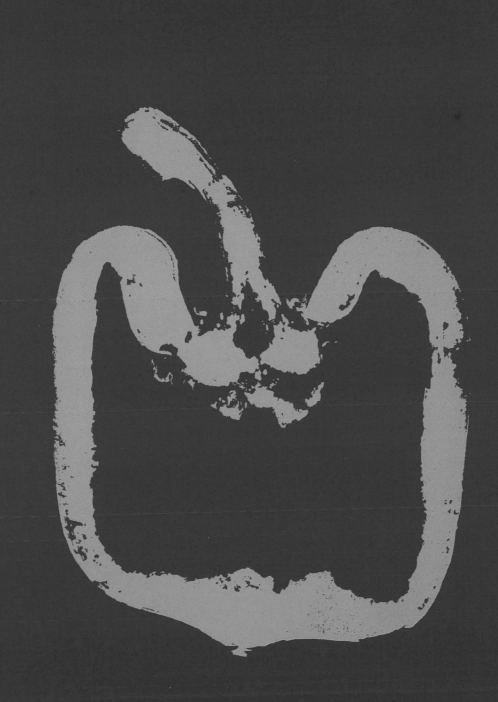

vegetables

Asian Herb Salad with Japanese Dressing

10 parts mixed lettuce

1 part Asian mixed herbs

Japanese dressing (see Basics Explained)

Wash and dry all the herbs and salad leaves and toss together with the dressing. Serve immediately.

Served as a side salad or a light meal topped with a piece of grilled fish, this flavourful salad is simply delicious. We use local Malaysian herbs such as daun kesum, daun pegagah, daun selasih and daun selom. They are mixed with salad leaves familiar in the Western world , for example lollo rosso, frisee and red batavia. The concept is similar to a French Mesclun but the Asian herbs give a totally new flavour experience. Explore your local markets and select a variety of herbs to use.

This is a very simple appetizer, it is essentially a snack food but also an interesting way to start a meal. Eda-mame is often served as a complimentary appetizer and is always popular. Serve with a beer or use the pods as a vegetable dish.

Eda-Mame (Japanese Soya Bean)

100 g (3½ oz) frozen eda-mame
200 ml (6½ fl oz) boiling water
1 tsp good quality sea salt flakes

Boil the beans from frozen for about 2 minutes or until they are hot inside, they do not need to be boiled for long, as they are sold precooked. Remove from water and drain well.

Sprinkle with the sea salt and toss.
Serve immediately.

Cherry Tomato and Kaffir Lime Leaf Salad

400 g (13 oz) red and yellow cherry tomatoes,
halved (preferably vine-ripened)

100 g (3½ oz) shallots, thinly sliced

10 kaffir lime leaves, deep-fried until crisp
then crumbled

6 tbsp extra virgin olive oil

2 tbsp lime juice

Sea salt

Freshly ground black pepper

Simply combine ingredients and toss.
Check and adjust seasoning to taste.

Adam wanted to add some green to a tomato salad and, having no basil left, used some crumbled, deep-fried kaffir lime leaves. During the photo shoot, one of us nibbled on the salad and discovered that it tasted as well as looked good.

While watching Bag Singh make vegetable samosas, the concept arose of making ravioli with a similar filling. As tandoori paneer was on hand, we chopped it up and used it as a filling. The resulting dish has been on our menus ever since.

Tandoori Paneer Vegetable Ravioli

FOR THE PASTA DOUGH

1200 g (2 lb 6½ oz) all-purpose flour

800 g (1 lb 10 oz) durum wheat flour

1½ tsp turmeric powder

1 tsp black onion seeds

1 tsp salt

20 eggs, 55 g (2 oz) each

2 tbsp cold water

120 ml (4 fl oz) extra virgin olive oil

FOR THE PANEER VEGETABLES

2 eggs, beaten

200 g (6½ oz) plain yoghurt, unsweetened

30 g (1 oz) chickpea flour

1 tsp fenugreek powder

800 g (1 lb 10 oz) paneer (an Indian cottage cheese), cut into 1 cm (½ in) cubes

3 medium onions, cut into 1 cm (½ in) cubes

5 tomatoes, cut into wedges

5 capsicums, red or yellow or a mixture of both, cut into 1 cm (½ in) cubes

1 tsp cumin seed, roasted

2 tsp garam masala

Salt

120 g (4 oz) whipping cream

To make the pasta, sieve the all-purpose flour and combine with the durum wheat flour, salt, turmeric and black onion seeds. Whisk the eggs and add the cold water to them. Mix well.

Make the dough by hand in the traditional way or use a dough mixer, which is recommended in this case. Add the flour mixture to the dough mixer, set controls to low speed and add the eggs slowly. Then add the olive oil and knead the dough until it is well mixed in. Remove, cover with cling film and place in the refrigerator for at least 2 hours before using.

To make the filling combine the eggs and yoghurt and whisk together. Add the chickpea flour and the fenugreek, and mix to form a paste. Add the paneer and all other ingredients and toss together well. Leave to marinate for about 1 hour. Preheat the oven to a very high heat, at least 240°C (465°F). Place the paneer vegetables on a tray, spread out evenly and bake for about 15 minutes. Remove, drain off the excess juices and leave to cool down. Chop to desired texture to use as a filling for the ravioli.

For the ravioli, roll out the dough to about 1 mm (1/16 in) thickness and brush with egg wash. Place little mounds of filling on the sheet, cover with another sheet and press down around the mounds. Cut out the ravioli with a cutter. Boil in rapidly boiling salted water for about 3 minutes, drain and serve. *Note:* The ravioli can be made in advance and frozen. When required, cook straight from frozen.

We serve it as a pasta dish in a curry lime broth, or as a main course topped with duck leg confit and some good duck jus.

Indian Spiced Eggplant

1 large round purple eggplant

1 tsp salt

1 litre (2 pints) vegetable oil for deep-frying

140 g (4½ oz) chapati flour
(whole wheat flour)

1 small onion, finely chopped

6 cloves garlic, minced

¼ tsp cayenne pepper

1 tsp ground coriander

1 tsp ground cumin

¼ tsp turmeric powder

200 g (6½ fl oz) coconut cream

2 tbsp chopped coriander leaves

Cut the eggplant into wedges. Place in a colander,
sprinkle with the salt and leave for 30 minutes.
Dry off excess liquid with a kitchen towel or paper.
Heat the oil for deep-frying.

Dust eggplant with the chapati flour and deep-fry
until golden brown. Remove and leave to drain on
absorbent paper.

In a large frying pan, heat some of the oil and sauté
the onions and garlic until the onions are transparent.
Add the spices and sautÈ for about 20 seconds
without burning the spices. Add the coconut cream
and simmer over slow heat until liquid is reduced
by half.

Add the eggplant and the chopped coriander, adjust
seasoning with salt and pepper if necessary and
serve immediately.

One of Bag Singh's simple but inspired ideas, this goes well with meat but is also good on its own. Any type of eggplant can be used.

The brief for this dish was to make a classic Western recipe using as many healthy and familiar Asian ingredients as possible. The result is a dish that is exceptionally popular because of its simplicity.

Asian Mushroom and Tofu Quiche

500 g (1 lb) short crust pastry

FOR THE MUSHROOMS

200 g (6½ oz) unsalted butter

1 medium onion, finely chopped

6 cloves garlic, finely chopped

1 kg (2 lb) assorted fresh Asian mushrooms (e.g. enoki shiitake, abalone, straw, shimeji)

100 ml (3½ fl oz) sake

Freshly ground black pepper

1 tbsp chopped mixed fresh herbs (chervil, basil, coriander, parsley)

FOR THE CUSTARD

12 free range eggs, about 55 g (2 oz) each

800 g (1 lb 10 oz) Japanese plain egg tofu

200 ml (6½ fl oz) low fat milk

1 tbsp light soya sauce

½ tbsp oyster sauce

Fish sauce for seasoning

Roll out the pastry dough and line a greased and floured pie pan. Add rice or baking pearls to it and bake blind at 180°C (355°F) for 15 minutes or until it is evenly baked and lightly coloured. Remove from oven and cool.

Heat the butter in a large frying pan and sauté the onions and garlic until they are transparent. Add the mushrooms and sauté until they are well cooked: this may need to be done in batches. Deglaze with the sake and season well with black pepper. Set aside to cool. Once the mushroom mixture is cold, toss the herbs through it.

In a blender, combine all the ingredients for the custard. Strain and leave to settle until bubbles disappear. Stir and season with the fish sauce.

Fill the quiche shell with the mushroom mixture and pour enough custard over to cover the mushrooms almost to the rim of the dough. Bake at 160°C (320°F) for about 30 minutes or until the quiche is cooked.

Serve with a fresh salad and maybe some sour cream with chives.

Roasted Pumpkin and Sweet Potatoes with Mustard Seeds and Chilli

60 g (2 oz) orange sweet potatoes,
peeled and cut into wedges

60 g (2 oz) purple sweet potatoes,
peeled and cut into wedges

60 g (2 oz) pumpkin, peeled,
seeds removed and cut into wedges

1 green chilli, seeds and stem removed
and cut into thick strips

1 red chilli, seeds and stem removed and
cut into thick strips

1 tsp black mustard seeds

2 tsp garam masala

16 shallots, peeled and left whole

120 ml (4 fl oz) olive oil

Salt and freshly ground black pepper

A few sprigs of coriander leaves for garnish

Combine all the ingredients except coriander and
mix until everything is well coated with oil.

Preheat the oven to 240°C (465°F). Preheat a roasting
pan and once hot add the vegetables to it. Roast for
about 10 minutes then scrape up the vegetables and
turn them over.

Roast until all the vegetables are well cooked.
Remove from the oven and adjust seasoning.

Serve immediately, garnished with the coriander leaves.

Originally invented as a side dish, this wonderful combination of flavours and colours has now gained the status of a vegetarian main course. Its simplicity is what makes it so good. Use only the best and freshest vegetables available.

Bubble and Squeak Dosei

FOR THE DOSEI

150 g (5 oz) urud dal (cleaned black lentils)

300 g (10 oz) long grain rice (Thai jasmine or similar)

½ tsp fenugreek

Salt, pepper and brown sugar

FOR THE BUBBLE AND SQUEAK

100 g (3½ oz) bacon, chopped

200 g (6½ oz) onions, sliced

150 g (5 oz) butter

500 g (1 lb) cabbage leaves, cooked and cut into 1 cm (½ in) squares

900 g (1 lb 13 oz) potatoes, cooked and coarsely mashed

Salt

Freshly ground pepper

100 ml (3½ fl oz) vegetable oil

Wash the rice and the lentils thoroughly in cold water at least three times. Cover them with cold water to about 5 cm (2 in) above, and leave to soak for 24 hours. Place into a blender together with the soaking water and the fenugreek, blend to a smooth, slightly thick batter. Season with salt, pepper and add a little brown sugar. Note that the batter should not taste sweet.

Cook the bacon and sliced onions in the butter until softened. Remove to a bowl and combine with all the other ingredients, except the oil. Season well. Heat the oil in a large frying pan and sauté the mixture for a couple of minutes until lightly browned. Remove from pan and keep hot.

Heat a large greased cast iron pan or Teflon pan. With a ladle make a thin crepe-like pancake with the dosei mixture. Brown on one side until the pancake is cooked through, turn quickly and cook for a few seconds on the other side.

Turn over again and place bubble and squeak filling on top. Roll up like a cone or a simple roll and serve. It must be served immediately so you get the combined textures of crispy pancake, soft mashed potatoes and crunchy cabbage.

Serve with a side salad or perhaps a lentil curry.

This dish shows how easily two cuisines can be merged. Dosei is a traditional Indian thin 'pancake', usually filled with curried potatoes. The idea of adding 'bubble and squeak' came one day when both things were on the menu — we decided to try this ever-so-English dish as a filling. It is a successful combination.

Lime Curry Leaf Rice

1½ litres (3 pints) water

500 g (1 lb) Thai jasmine fragrant rice

300 ml (10 fl oz) lime juice

10 kaffir lime leaves

8 curry leaves

6 stalks lemon grass, smashed

6 cardamom pods, cracked

Rinse the rice until water runs clear. Bring water to the boil and add rice and all other ingredients, stir well. Reduce heat, bring to a simmer and cover with a lid. Leave over low heat until the rice is cooked. This should take about 15 minutes, depending on the rice used. Remove lid and fluff up the rice.

Butter can be added, or a sprinkling of spring onions, fried shallots or garlic.

When Peng told me about this recipe, at first I did not believe that lime and rice would work together. Yet this simple dish is wonderfully fragrant and tasty. It can be served plain, and it also goes particularly well with fish or chicken dishes.

Black Glutinous Rice and Crunchy Vegetable Salad with Roasted Cashew Nuts

FOR THE SALAD

300 g (10 oz) crunchy cooked or raw vegetables of your choice – the more colours and textures the better

100 ml (3½ fl oz) extra virgin olive oil

60 g (2 oz) roasted cashew nuts

2 large bunches of fresh coriander, coarsely chopped

1 bunch fresh mint, chopped

1 piece ginger, finely grated, placed in muslin cloth and juice squeezed out

Juice of 3 limes

Tabasco

Salt and freshly ground black pepper

FOR THE RICE

2 cups black glutinous rice

4 cups water

2 cloves garlic

1 piece ginger

1 tsp salt

2 stalks lemon grass

2 chilli padi

Wash the rice thoroughly, cover with water and leave to soak for 2 to 3 hours then drain.

Combine all the ingredients for the rice in a pot and simmer over medium heat until the rice is cooked. Drain and rinse the rice to remove gluten. Remove and discard the other ingredients.

Combine all the salad ingredients and toss well with the rice, adjust seasoning to taste.

Add some chilli if liked. I use tomatoes, carrots, onions, capsicums, sweet sugar peas, watercress, pea shoots and fennel to make this salad.

As black glutinous rice is normally served as a dessert, I was amazed when Peng served me a savoury dish made from it. This salad is packed with contrasting flavours, colours and textures — it is everything good food should be.

Anton Mosimann stated in his book *Fish Cuisine* that when people ask what he most likes to eat and to cook, his answer is always fish — which he would expand on to include seafood.

I would make the same statement. *Fish (and seafood)* make a cook look good; the qualities of this wonderful food are attributed to the cook. It is versatile in its variety, size, consistency, taste and texture, and it can be prepared using almost every imaginable cooking method. In addition, fish and seafood can be paired with endless varieties of vegetables and sauces, even other protein items. It is therefore not surprising that this section has the most recipes.

fish and seafood

Bean curd skin is a by-product of tofu production; it is the skin that forms when the bean curd is steamed. It is removed, in sheets, from the bean curd itself and dried to make bean curd skin. This is a very versatile product, which lends itself to stuffing with a range of fillings. Here it is wrapped around a crab mixture to make 'cannelloni'. It adds crunchy texture to the dish. In this recipe, the 'cannelloni' is served with a curry lime broth; but it can be eaten by itself with a squeeze of fresh lime.

Asian Mud Crab Cannelloni with Curry Lime Broth

FOR THE CANNELLONI FILLING

20 g (¾ oz) unsalted butter

1 tbsp olive oil

½ small onion, finely diced

1 chilli padi, sliced

250 g (8 oz) fresh mud crab meat, or any other fresh crab meat

½ tsp Togarashi spice

Salt and pepper

20 g (¾ oz) Parmesan cheese

1 small boiled potato, mashed

120 g (4 oz) thick béchamel sauce (see Basics Explained)

2 tsp chopped fresh coriander leaves

FOR THE CURRY LIME BROTH (SAUCE)

4 tbsp olive oil

2 tsp curry powder

2½ cm (1 in) piece galangal, sliced

1 small onion, chopped

5 shallots, chopped

4 sprigs of curry leaves

2 kaffir lime leaves

2½ cm (1 in) piece old ginger, sliced

1 large medium-hot chilli, chopped

1½ litres (3 pints) Asian chicken stock (see Basics Explained)

220 ml (7 fl oz) coconut cream

Juice of 1 lime

Thai or Vietnamese fish sauce to season

FOR THE CANNELLONI

12 sheets bean curd skin, soaked and softened

2 litres (4 pints) oil for deep-frying

Over medium heat, combine the butter and olive oil in a pan and sauté the onion and chilli padi until the onion is transparent.

Add the crab meat and season with salt, pepper and Togarashi spice. Sauté for about 1 minute, then place into a bowl and add all the other filling ingredients. Mix well until all ingredients are evenly combined. Check the seasoning once more and leave to cool down.

When the filling is cold, spread flat the sheets of bean curd skin and fill with the crab meat mixture. Roll as you would a large spring roll, making sure the ends are sealed. You can seal the skin with a little flour and water paste on the edges. Deep-fry in a large wok or pot over moderate heat. Do not put too many cannelloni in at once. Deep-fry the cannelloni until they are golden brown all over. Remove from the oil and leave to drain on absorbent paper.

Before serving, place in a preheated oven at 180°C (355°F) for 3 or 4 minutes to heat thoroughly. For the sauce, heat the olive oil and fry all the spices, herbs, chilli and shallots for about 1 minute over moderate heat until the ingredients release their fragrance. Add the stock and half the coconut cream. Leave to simmer for about 20 minutes.

Add the remaining coconut cream and reduce slowly to a good sauce texture. Strain and season with lime juice and fish sauce to taste. Serve with the cannelloni.

Hot-Smoked Apricot Salmon on a Soba Noodle-Enoki Mushroom Salad with a Mirin-Ponzu Dressing

FOR THE SALMON

1 tbsp sunflower oil

1 tbsp finely chopped shallots

3 tsp finely minced ginger

½ cup finely diced dried apricots

2 tbsp white wine vinegar

2 tbsp white wine

2 tbsp apricot jam

4 fresh salmon fillets about 80 -140 g (3 - 5 oz) each, depending on whether served as an appetizer or a main course

FOR THE MIRIN-PONZU DRESSING

5 tsp mirin

1 tbsp ponzu (a Japanese sauce, available bottled)

4 tbsp extra virgin olive oil

Freshly ground black pepper

FOR THE NOODLE SALAD

120 g (4 oz) soba noodles (more, if served as a main course)

50 g (2 oz) enoki mushrooms, roots cut off (more, if served as a main course)

1 tbsp extra virgin olive oil

Small bunch of watercress

1 tsp chopped chives

FOR THE GARNISH

6 tbsp tomato-herb mixture (see Basics Explained)

Toasted white and black sesame seeds

For the apricot marinade, first sauté the shallots and ginger in sunflower oil over medium heat until the shallots are transparent but not coloured. Add the dried apricots and sauté briefly.

Deglaze with the vinegar, reduce slightly, and then add the wine. Reduce the wine by half before adding the jam. Simmer for 10 -15 minutes, then remove from the heat and leave to cool. If the mixture is lumpy, place in a food blender and blend to a smooth paste. Spread this mixture evenly over the salmon about 2 hours before smoking.

To prepare the salmon, clean and trim before coating with the marinade. If using a smoker, cold smoke the salmon for 5 minutes before removing. Bake at 180°C (355°F) for about 5 minutes, depending on the thickness of the salmon. For a stove-top smoker, place salmon inside, add wood shavings to the base, and smoke for 3 minutes. Then remove and finish by baking in the same way as described earlier. The taste of the smoke should be subtle, not dominant.

To make the dressing, place all the ingredients in a bowl and mix well. For the noodle salad, bring a pot of salted water to a boil and quickly blanch the soba noodles. Do not overcook them; they only need a few minutes to cook. Drain noodles well.

In a frying pan, quickly sauté the enoki mushrooms in olive oil without adding much colour to them. Combine the noodles with the enoki mushrooms, mirin-ponzu dressing, chives and watercress. Toss well to mix.

Serve the hot salmon on top of the cold salad and add a generous spoonful of the tomato-herb mixture. Sprinkle with toasted sesame seeds.

Aquatas in Tasmania is a leading producer of unique, high quality salmon products. Their hot-smoked apricot salmon inspired this recipe; it can be used to make this dish if smoking apparatus is not available.

SOUTH TYNESIDE COLLEGE

RESOURCE CENTRE

Japanese spices and seasonings have unique characteristics, some are very pungent, some subtle. Togarashi, a Japanese spice blend of chilli, sesame, seaweed and orange peel, is used as a seasoning in soups, noodle dishes and in general to add spice to a dish. Tabasco sauce is used in a similar manner in the Western world. A Cajun soft-shell crab dish served at the Drake Hotel in Chicago inspired this recipe. I added a lemon grass risotto and braised spring onions to give more texture to the dish. Serve this dish as an appetizer or main course, or serve the crab and risotto separately. If soft-shell crabs are not available, replace them with a similar quantity of prawns.

Togarashi Soft-Shell Crab on Lemon Grass Risotto with Braised Spring Onions

FOR THE RISOTTO

2 tbsp extra virgin olive oil

2 shallots, finely chopped

400 ml (13 fl oz) sake

400 ml (13 fl oz) dry white wine

3 tbsp lemon grass water
(see Basics Explained)

60 g (2 oz) risotto rice

500 ml (1 pint) Asian chicken stock
(see Basics Explained)

40 g (1½ oz) butter

40 g (1½ oz) grated Parmesan cheese

Freshly ground black pepper

FOR THE BRAISED SPRING ONIONS

40 g (1½ oz) unsalted butter

12 young spring onions

400 ml (13 fl oz) Asian chicken stock
(see Basics Explained)

1 tsp sugar

Salt and pepper

A few leaves Italian (sweet) basil,
finely chopped

FOR THE CRABS

4 soft-shell crabs

2 tsp Togarashi spice

50 g (2 oz) plain flour, for dusting the crabs

Salt, if required

1 litre (2 pints) vegetable oil for deep-frying
(do not use olive oil here, it is too strongly
flavoured to use with crab)

*Note: If you want to serve this as a complete dish, you
must make the risotto first, the onions second, and the
soft-shell crabs last. If not, follow the steps individually.*

To make the risotto, first sauté the shallots in olive oil, and then de-glaze the pan with the sake, wine and finally the lemon grass water. Add risotto rice and stock (see Basics Explained for method). Finish off with pepper, butter and Parmesan cheese.

To prepare the spring onions, butter a pan and place the spring onions inside. Season with sugar, salt and pepper and put a few knobs of butter on top. Add chicken stock and cover the whole pan with grease-proof paper. Place in a moderate oven at for about 10 minutes or until the spring onions are well cooked. To finish, gently toss the chopped basil with the spring onions. Make sure the crabs are cleaned and washed, be sure to remove the lungs beneath the top shell, but do not break the crabs apart.

Heat the oil to about 180-190°C (355-375°F), preferably in a large wok so that there is ample space for the crabs to be surrounded by plenty of hot oil. This will ensure they turn out evenly crispy. Season the crabs with a little salt (if necessary). Dust them well with flour mixed with half the Togarashi spice. Deep-fry crabs until they are crispy. Remove and place on absorbent paper to soak up the excess oil and season again with remaining Togarashi spice.

Serve crabs on their own, or with risotto and spring onions.

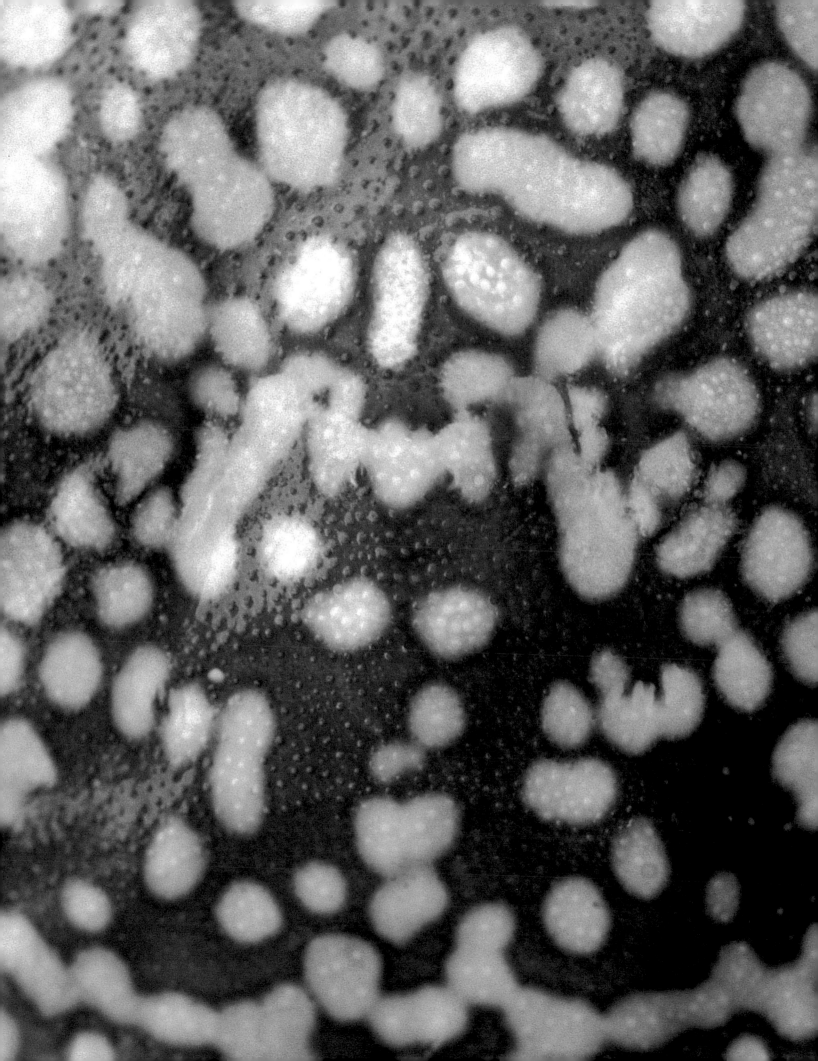

Kataifi Prawns

FOR THE TOBIKO MAYONNAISE

4 tbsp mayonnaise (see Basics Explained)

2 tsp lime juice

1 tsp orange tobiko (Japanese flying fish roe)

1 tsp wasabi tobiko (Japanese flying fish roe)

Zest of ½ lime, finely chopped

½ kaffir lime leaf, finely chopped

Salt and pepper

FOR THE PRAWNS

10 tiger prawns, peeled, de-veined, tail on.
Size should be about 20 per kg (10 per lb)

1 packet kataifi dough, also sold as
shredded filo pastry

1 litre (2 pints) vegetable oil for deep-frying

To make the tobiko mayonnaise combine all the
ingredients and season with salt and pepper.
Wrap the prawns with the kataifi dough, so that
you have a good layer of dough wrapped around
everything except the tail.

Heat the oil to about 180°C (355°F) and deep-fry the
prawns until they are golden brown. Remove and
drain on absorbent paper.

Serve immediately with tobiko mayonnaise.

Inventing an original prawn recipe is a challenge. When we were developing recipes for the Post Bar snack menu, MPS Puri suggested wrapping prawns in kataifi. It works very well and gives this dish an interesting texture.

Chinese-Style Crispy Fried Pomfret with Suen-Lat sauce

FOR THE SAUCE (STAGE 1)

5 cm (2 in) piece galangal, sliced

60 g (2 oz) chilli paste

20 chilli padi

8 shallots, chopped

120 ml (4 fl oz) tamarind water (see Basics Explained)

15 cm (6 in) piece fresh turmeric, sliced

60 g (2 oz) candlenuts

1 tbsp dried shrimps

60 g (2 oz) tom yam paste

4 tsp oyster sauce

3 stalks lemon grass, lightly crushed

FOR THE SAUCE (STAGE 2)

8 kaffir lime leaves

80 g (3 oz) sugar

1 piece ginger flower

1 tsp dry shrimp paste (belacan)

1 tbsp chilli powder

30 g (1 oz) brown bean paste

2 tbsp lemon juice

1 tbsp lime juice

1 large tomato, skinned, seeds removed and finely diced

FOR THE FISH

4 whole pomfret, gutted and cleaned - about 350 grams (11 oz) each

1 tbsp fish sauce

3 cups rice flour or tempura flour

4 litres (8 pints) vegetable oil for deep-frying

Note: The sauce can be prepared ahead of time, by as much as a day in advance. Avoid keeping it too long as it will lose flavour.

For Stage 1 of the sauce, combine all the ingredients and bring to a simmer. Gently simmer for about 20 minutes but not longer. At the same time, in another pot, combine the ingredients for Stage 2 and cook over low heat for about 15 minutes. Do not cook for longer than 15 minutes as the bitter essence of the lime leaves will be released. Combine all the ingredients of Stage 1 and Stage 2 and blend until you have a smooth sambal-style paste.

Now prepare the fish. Deeply score the flesh in a criss-cross pattern, leaving about a 1½ cm (¾ in) space between each cut. Brush over with the fish sauce, then dredge the fish in flour and shake off any excess.

Heat the oil in a wok or pot that is large and deep enough to comfortably accommodate two fish at a time. Over medium-high heat deep-fry the fish, taking care not to overcook. Constantly turn the fish over and move them around the wok or pot to ensure they become an even golden brown. Remove and place on absorbent paper. Keep hot until all the fish are cooked, and then serve immediately.

Serve the sauce as a dip, or mix it with a Western-style lemon butter sauce and pour over the fish. The fish may be accompanied by a stir-fry of bean sprouts, red capsicum and pea sprouts.

The Chinese method of deep-frying whole fish comes as a surprise to most Western chefs. It is important to score the fish right down to the bone in a criss-cross pattern, and to fry it at moderate to high heat in a large container (preferably a wok) with lots of oil. Although several types of fish are prepared this way, pomfret is one of the most suitable. It is also difficult as it can quickly overcook. Suen-Lat sauce is a traditional Chinese sour and spicy sauce.

Parrot Fish Wrapped in Bean Curd Skin

4 sprigs coriander leaves, chopped

4 tbsp oyster sauce

4 parrot fish fillets, skinned and de-boned, about 140 grams (4½ oz) each

Salt and freshly ground black pepper

4 sheets bean curd skin, soaked and softened

1 litre (2 pints) vegetable oil

Combine the chopped coriander leaves with the oyster sauce. Season the fish lightly with salt and pepper, and brush all over with the oyster sauce mixture. Wrap the fish in bean curd skin as you would wrap a parcel, moistening the edges to make sure it is well sealed.

Heat the oil to medium-hot, preferably in a wok, and deep-fry the fish until it is cooked through and the skin is golden brown. Serve immediately.

I serve this dish on a stir-fry of endive, sugar snap peas and orange segments with a citrus-coriander sauce.

This dish uses the concept of wrapping bean curd skin around a filling, an idea copied from Ken Hom.
The deep-fried parcels must be served as soon as they come out of the oil, or the stunning texture will be spoiled.

Pan-Seared Black Cod Fillet with a Sun-Dried Tomato Sambal, XO Sauce and Miso Jus

FOR THE MISO JUS

2 tbsp fish stock (see Basics Explained)

120 ml (4 fl oz) veal stock (see Basics Explained)

30 g (1 oz) dark miso paste

2 tsp cold butter, cut into pieces

FOR THE COD

4 tbsp olive oil

4 Arctic black cod fillets, 150 g (5 oz) each

salt and pepper

160 g (6 oz) baby kailan or choy tam

2 tbsp unsalted butter

120 g (4 oz) fresh lily bulbs

12 red or yellow cherry tomatoes or mixture of both, halved

2 tbsp sun-dried tomato sambal (see Basics Explained)

1 tbsp XO sauce (see Basics Explained)

To make the miso jus first simmer the fish stock to reduce it by half. Then add the veal stock, and again reduce by about half (depending on concentration required).

Next, stir in the miso paste and the pieces of butter. Do not let it boil again as both the miso and the butter will cause the sauce to separate. Adjust the seasoning if necessary.

Heat the olive oil in a cast-iron or Teflon pan, almost to smoking point. Season the cod with salt and pepper and place into the hot pan. Sear it on one side for about 4 minutes. Turn over and pan-roast the other side until cooked. The fish should be flaky and moist when you part the flesh.

Remove from the pan and leave to rest in a warm place for about 5 minutes. Before serving, reheat for 20 seconds in a very hot oven at 240°C (465°F). Blanch the baby kailan or choy tam quickly in boiling water, remove and drain. Melt the butter in a sauté pan or wok. Add the lily bulbs and sauté for about 20 seconds. Add the warm blanched vegetables and cherry tomatoes, season and toss well until the tomatoes begin to wilt.

To serve, drizzle a little XO sauce on a plate and top with the vegetables. Arrange the cod on the vegetables and put a dollop of sambal on the top. Finally, spoon some jus around the presentation and serve immediately.

This is undoubtedly the best dish I have ever created. It was inspired by an excellent meal at Cilantro in Kuala Lumpur. Ken, the Malaysian Chinese chef at the time, had previously worked with two of Australia's best 'fusion' chefs, Neil Perry and Tetsuya Wakuda. This dish is a *vivid combination of robust flavours, textures and colours.*

Stir-Fried Seafood with Assorted Vegetables

30 g (1 oz) red capsicum, cut into strips

30 g (1 oz) green capsicum, cut into strips

60 g (2 oz) zucchini, sliced

30 g (1 oz) sugar snap peas

30 g (1 oz) green runner beans

30 g (1 oz) baby corn

60 g (2 oz) choy tam or baby kailan

30 g (1 oz) water chestnuts, sliced

30 g (1 oz) siew pak choy or any other pak choy

100 ml (3 fl oz) corn oil

1 tsp sesame oil

8 cloves garlic, sliced

15 cm (6 in) piece ginger, minced

1 stalk lemon grass, minced

4 shallots, sliced

4 chillies, finely chopped

6 curry leaves

10 kaffir lime leaves, finely chopped

800 g (1lb 10 oz) assorted fish and seafood, cut into bite-size pieces (use firm-fleshed fish)

4 tbsp Shao Xing wine

Fish sauce

Light soy sauce

Finely ground white pepper

60 g (2 oz) roasted cashew nuts

Quickly blanch and drain all the vegetables before stir-frying them.

Heat the oil in a wok and add the garlic, ginger, shallots, lemon grass, chilli, curry and lime leaves. Sauté over low heat until fragrant.

Add all the vegetables and seafood and toss well. Increase the heat to high and add the Shao Xing wine.

Next, season to taste with the fish sauce, soy sauce and white pepper. Stir-fry until all the vegetables are completely heated through.

Add the cashew nuts and toss again. Serve immediately.

This is a fusion version of a classic Chinese one-dish meal. As a variation Malay ingredients are added, any combination of seafood and vegetables can be used.

Chinese, Japanese and Western influences come together beautifully in this simple dish. Live prawns are best for this — the texture is superb.

Fresh River Prawns Chinese-Style with Kaffir Lime Mayonnaise

FOR THE MAYONNAISE

1 litre (2 pints) sunflower oil

8 stalks lemon grass, lightly crushed

10 kaffir lime leaves

7 egg yolks

120 ml (4 fl oz) ponzu (a Japanese sauce, available bottled)

1 tbsp Dijon mustard

salt and pepper

FOR THE SAUCE (TO TOSS WITH PRAWNS)

100 ml (3½ fl oz) light soya sauce

4 tsp Shao Xing wine

2 tbsp Asian chicken stock (see Basics Explained)

1 tbsp sugar

24 live river prawns, 20/30 per kg (10/15 per lb)

To make the mayonnaise, first add the lemon grass and lime leaves to the oil. Leave it over a low heat to infuse for 2 or 3 hours, without frying the ingredients. Strain and set aside to cool. Use this oil to prepare the mayonnaise as instructed in the Basics Explained section, with the addition of ponzu. Season with salt and pepper and chill until needed.

Combine all the ingredients for the sauce and keep aside until needed.

In a large pot, bring to a rapid boil sufficient water to cook the prawns – about three times the volume of prawns. (A high-powered wok-burner is best for this.)

Next, add the prawns to the boiling water and cook for 3 minutes or slightly longer, depending on the size of the prawns. As soon as they are cooked, remove from the water, drain and toss with the sauce.

Serve immediately with ponzu mayonnaise on the side.

Every year, when the mussel season began in late September, my parents would take me to sample the first arrivals at a local restaurant. In Germany, mussels make up a complete meal. The stock is the soup course, the mussels form the main course, and bread is always served with the meal. This recipe, which combines a typical North European dish with an Asian cooking method and Asian ingredients, is a fine example of trans-ethnic cuisine. I prefer black mussels to the NZ green-lipped variety, as they are juicier and more tender. In the US, mussels from Kamilche are popular.

Wok-Steamed Mussels with Shao Xing Wine and Chinese Celery

4 tbsp extra virgin olive oil

1 medium Maui onion (or other mild sweet onion), finely diced

1 carrot, finely diced

1 bunch Chinese celery, cleaned and chopped into 1 cm (½ in) pieces

1 tsp grated galangal

1 kaffir lime leaf

1 kg (2 lb) live black mussels

4 tbsp fish stock or water

4 tbsp Shao Xing wine

Zest of 1 lime

1 medium tomato, skinned, seeds removed and cut into large dice

Salt or fish sauce

Freshly ground black pepper

½ bunch fresh coriander leaves

In a wok, heat the olive oil over medium heat and sauté the onion, carrot, celery, galangal and kaffir lime leaf for about 1 minute.

Then add the mussels and stir well. Increase the heat to high and keep stirring. After 10-15 seconds add the fish stock or water and half of the Shao Xing wine. Cover with a lid and leave to steam for 2 minutes.

Add the lime zest and toss the mussels well. Next, add the tomato and cover again for a further minute or until the mussels are steamed open. When the shells open, the mussels are cooked; reduce the heat to low.

Add the rest of the Shao Xing wine. Season with salt or fish sauce and some freshly ground pepper.

Garnish with coriander leaves and serve immediately with some crusty bread on the side.

Crispy Black Cod Fillet with Spicy Mango Salsa

FOR THE SPICY MANGO SALSA

1 medium tomato, seeds removed and cut into strips

1 mango (semi-ripe), peeled and cut into strips

1 medium red onion or 4 large red shallots, cut into thin strips

½ bunch coriander leaves, coarsely chopped

2 kaffir lime leaves, cut into thin strips

2 tsp finely chopped galangal

1 large red chilli, seeds and stem removed, cut into thin strips

4 tbsp Thai chilli sauce

2 tsp rice vinegar

2 tbsp sugar

2 tsp fish sauce

Juice of 1 lime

FOR THE COD

4 black cod fillets, skin on, about 150 g (5 oz) each

Salt and pepper

4 tbsp cornflour

2 litres (4 pints) vegetable oil for deep-frying

For the mango salsa, combine all ingredients in a bowl and mix well. Adjust seasoning with fish sauce and some extra lime juice if necessary.

Cut insertions into the cod diagonally across, from the flesh side down towards the skin. Do not cut through the skin but stop about ½ cm (¼ in) before. Make the cuts about 1 cm (½ in) apart, and then do the same in the other direction to form a criss-cross pattern. This will ensure that the cod will be crispy yet juicy. Season with salt and pepper. Coat the cod with the cornflour.

Heat the oil, preferably in a wok, to about 200°C (390°F). Deep-fry cod fillets until crisp and golden brown, remove from the oil and place on absorbent paper to remove excess oil.

Serve the cod topped with the mango salsa. It can be accompanied by steamed rice.

Chef Sam Leong developed this dish for the Town restaurant at The Fullerton. It combines wonderful textures and flavours and is extremely vivid on the palate. Sam's innovative food is often inspired by Thai cuisine.

Bagel Sushi Roll

1 piece yaki nori (dry seaweed for
making sushi rolls)

100 g (3½ oz) sushi rice
(see Basics Explained)

1 tsp wasabi

25 g (1 oz) fresh salmon, trimmed and
cut into finger-sized strips

15 g (½ oz) cream cheese, cut into
sticks similar in size to the salmon

1 tsp black and white sesame seeds,
toasted

1 shallot, finely chopped

1 lemon, cut into wedges

Lay the yaki nori on a bamboo sushi mat, place the
rice on top and spread out evenly. Brush the wasabi
over the rice then place the salmon and the cream
cheese together along one side of the rice layer.
Roll up, holding the bamboo mat firmly to obtain a
tight roll.

Remove sushi from mat and roll in the toasted
sesame seeds to coat.

Cut into 6 equal pieces and serve with the chopped
shallots, lemon wedges and some breadsticks.

Although not Japanese by birth, Eugene is a traditional Japanese chef, trained by master chefs. He is, however, open-minded with regard to non-traditional foods. After hearing about lox and bagel, he created this Japanese version of the famous combination.

NORTH TYNESIDE COLLEGE

LEARNING RESOURCE CENTRE

Black Squid Risotto with Sake, Chilli Padi and Coriander

FOR THE RISOTTO

2 chilli padi, seeds and stem removed, sliced

2 bunches coriander roots

4 tbsp finely chopped coriander leaves

100 g (3½ oz) unsalted butter

10 shallots, finely chopped

150 g (5 fl oz) arborio rice

200 ml (6½ fl oz) sake

100 ml (3½ fl oz) dry white wine

4 tbsp pasteurised squid ink

1200 ml (2 pints 6½ fl oz) Asian chicken or fish stock (see Basics Explained)

50 g (2 oz) Parmesan cheese

FOR THE SQUID

4 tbsp extra virgin olive oil

4 shallots, chopped

1 clove garlic, finely chopped

240 g (8 oz) squid, cleaned and sliced into ½ cm (¼ in) rings

3 tbsp dry white wine

2 tbsp sake

Juice of 1 or 2 limes

1 small tomato, skinned, seeds removed and diced

2 tbsp finely chopped coriander leaves

salt and freshly ground black pepper

30 g (1 oz) unsalted butter

Cook the risotto as described in Basics Explained, starting with the chilli and the coriander root. Then add the coriander leaves and continue with the cooking process, using the ingredients listed.

When risotto is almost ready, cook the squid. Heat the olive oil in a large sauté pan or frying pan and sauté the shallots and garlic until transparent. Add the squid and sauté for about a minute. Then add the wine, sake and lime juice, and simmer for about 30 seconds. Add the tomato, chopped coriander leaves and seasoning.

Stir well and check that the squid is cooked. Do not overcook the squid, as it will become tough. To finish, stir in the butter.

Serve the risotto in a bowl and place the squid on top.

This dish features vividly contrasting colours: shiny black risotto with pinkish-white squid, green coriander and red tomatoes. The combination of tastes and textures is just as vivid. Use fresh squid ink if possible, pasteurised with red wine. It has a sweet taste that gives body to the dish. In Asia fresh squid is readily available in all sizes, it is a versatile seafood that is often underestimated.

Crispy and light yet filling, with a multitude of flavours: this is the perfect lunch dish. Local farmed seabass is used here, but it works just as well with red mullet or snapper.

Indian Spiced Seabass Fillet on Curried Lentil Hash

8 tbsp olive oil

4 seabass fillets, skin on, about 150 g (5 oz) each (ask your fishmonger to scale and fillet it)

2 tbsp Indian Spice Mixture (see Basics Explained)

120 g (4 oz) good quality unsalted butter

1 medium potato, peeled and cut into ½ cm (¼ in) cubes

4 shallots, finely chopped

1 garlic clove, finely chopped

2 tbsp each red lentils, black lentils, yellow lentils, brown lentils and chickpeas – pre-boiled (see Cooking Pulses in Basics Explained)

10 curry leaves, finely chopped

2 tsp turmeric powder

2 tsp curry powder

8 tbsp tomato-herb mixture (see Basics Explained)

chervil or coriander leaves

Take a large frying pan, preferably cast-iron, and heat 3 tbsp olive oil to almost smoking point. Season the seabass fillet on both sides with the Indian Spice Mixture. Ease the seabass fillet, skin side down, into the hot oil. Reduce heat to moderate and pan-fry on the skin side until the fish is almost completely cooked through.

When the sides are opaque white with only the surface of the fish uncooked, add 60 g (2 oz) of butter to the pan and turn the fillets over to finish. This will take no longer then a minute.

Remove the fish immediately from the pan and set aside in a warm place until needed. Do not leave for longer than 5 minutes, which is approximately the time needed to make the lentil hash.

In a large frying pan, heat 4 tbsp olive oil to almost smoking and shallow-fry the potato until cooked and well browned on all sides. Remove from the pan, drain off excess oil and keep aside. Take another large frying pan (or the one the fish was cooked in) and, over moderate heat, add 60 g (2 oz) of butter mixed with 1 tbsp of olive oil. Add the shallots and garlic to this. Once the shallots are transparent, reduce the heat and add the curry leaves, turmeric and curry powder. Sauté for about 1 minute to release the fragrance of the spices and curry leaves.

Then add the potatoes and lentils and sauté until the mixture is completely heated through. Season with salt and pepper and add more butter if the hash is too dry.

Arrange the fish and curried lentil hash on individual plates or a serving platter, and serve with the tomato-herb mixture. Garnish with chervil or coriander leaves.

Mud Crab Salad with Coconut-Lime Dressing

When a local magazine asked us to be creative with crabs, Adam produced this wonderful salad on the spot. If you live in a country with a seasonal climate, it is an ideal summer dish.

FOR THE DRESSING

100 ml (3½ fl oz) lime juice

2 tbsp rice wine vinegar

2 tbsp fish sauce

1 tbsp sugar

½ tsp sesame oil

100 ml (3½ fl oz) olive oil

2 tbsp coconut milk

Freshly ground black pepper

FOR THE SALAD

500 g (1 lb) mud crab meat (or other crab meat; deep-fried soft-shell crabs are also suitable)

6 spring onions, finely sliced

1 large red chilli, seeds removed and sliced

1 tbsp Chinese pickled ginger, sliced into strips

½ Asian cucumber, seeds removed and cut into strips

½ daikon radish, peeled and sliced into ribbons

2 tbsp roasted cashew nuts

2 tomatoes, skinned, seeds removed and finely diced

1 bunch fresh enoki mushrooms, roots cut off

½ tbsp chopped coriander leaves

8 kaffir lime leaves, deep fried and crumbled

4 shallots, finely sliced

5 tbsp deep-fried shallots (crispy fried shallots are available in jars or packets)

140 g (4½ oz) rocket greens

Combine all the ingredients for the dressing and whisk well. Adjust seasoning with some freshly ground black pepper and, if necessary, more fish sauce.

Next, combine all the salad ingredients and add half the dressing. Toss well and taste for seasoning. Add more dressing to suit, the quantity required depends on the liquid in the crab and other ingredients. Serve immediately.

The significance of *poultry* in ethnic food around the world is astounding. Christmas and Thanksgiving turkeys, Peking duck, chicken curries, barbecue chicken wings, steamed chicken's feet – these are not only popular but also highly significant dishes in their respective cultures. *Meat* also plays a major role in most cuisines. As meat and poultry are very important sources of protein, it is essential always to use the best available quality.

"The significance of poultry in ethnic food around the world is astounding."

meat and poulty

Asian-Style Duck Leg Confit on a Chinese Herbal Risotto

12 duck legs, with good meat and fat content

300 g (10 oz) coarse sea salt

2 litres (4 pints) melted duck fat

2 pieces ginger flower stem

2 stalks lemon grass, crushed

1 kaffir lime leaf

2 - 4 chilli padi

1 bunch coriander roots

12 portions Chinese herbal risotto (see Risotto recipe in Basics Explained, use Black Chicken Herbal Broth – see Soups and Laksa – as cooking liquid)

400 ml (13 fl oz) duck sauce (see Basics Explained)

Mix the duck legs and coarse sea salt together until well combined and cover with a tea towel. Refrigerate for 12 -14 hours. Remove the duck from the salt and wipe off the excess salt and salty juices with a cloth.

Take a pot that can easily hold the 12 duck legs and still leave a 15 cm (6 in) space to the rim.

Pour in the duck fat; add the duck legs and all the other ingredients. Place over a low heat and leave to simmer very slowly for about 1½ hours, skimming the surface occasionally. To test if the meat is cooked take a wooden skewer and pierce it. If it goes through like butter then the duck is perfectly cooked.

Remove the duck legs, strain the fat and pour back on top of the duck, leave it to cool in the fat. Then remove duck from the fat and leave the fat to settle for about 2 hours. Ladle the pure fat on to the duck meat making sure the fat runs in between the pieces. Be sure not to ladle out any of the juice, which should have separated to the bottom of the fat, or the duck will not keep.

Keep the confit in a cool place until the next day, and then cover with greaseproof paper until needed. Refrigeration is not necessary as long as there is no juice mixed in with the duck and fat.

To reheat, remove the number of legs needed and bake them in the oven until hot; or reheat in some duck fat. Finish off under a grill or broiler to make crisp.

Serve on Chinese herbal risotto with duck sauce.

This is a variation of the superb confit served by Pierre Koffmann at La Tante Claire. Adam added lemon grass, chilli, kaffir lime leaf, ginger flower and coriander root to the classic recipe to give a subtle Asian flavour. Serve with noodles or rice. When paired with a Chinese herbal risotto the mix of flavours is wonderful.

Trans-ethnic cuisine marriages do not happen easily. This is the shared effort of myself, Adam and my Executive Sous Chef Thierry Marais. Here you have a Chinese poultry preparation combined with a traditional Middle Eastern salad.

Soya-Ginger Marinated Quail with Spicy Tabouleh Salad

FOR THE SOYA-GINGER MARINADE

4 tbsp sugar

1 tsp salt

½ tsp five spice powder

½ tsp ground ginger

15 cm (6 in) piece ginger, peeled and finely chopped

3 pieces star anise

½ bay leaf

200 ml (6½ fl oz) light soya sauce

1 tbsp Chinese red vinegar

2 tbsp rice wine

2 tbsp rice vinegar

12 quails, cut in half

2 litres (4 pints) vegetable oil for deep-frying

FOR THE TABOULEH

120 g (4 oz) burghul (cracked wheat)

40 g (1½ oz) diced tomato flesh

40 g (1½ oz) cucumber, seeds removed and diced

6 chilli padi, finely chopped

40 ml (1½ fl oz) fresh lemon juice, or more

2 tbsp chopped flat parsley

3 cloves garlic, minced

80 ml (3 fl oz) extra virgin olive oil

1 tbsp tomato juice

Tabasco

Salt and freshly ground pepper

Combine all the ingredients for the marinade and bring to a simmer, remove from the heat and leave to cool. Add the quails and leave to marinate for 6 hours in the refrigerator.

Place the burghul in a bowl large enough to hold 5 times its volume. Boil 1 litre (2 pints) of water and pour over the burghul. Leave to soak for about 3 hours. Drain well and dry on a kitchen towel. Combine the burghul with all other ingredients and season well; it should be slightly sour and a bit spicy.

Remove quails from marinade and bake them in a roasting pan at 220°C (425°F) for about 15 minutes. Remove from the oven. Bring the oil to moderate heat. Deep-fry the quails in small batches until they are just golden brown and crispy. Do not leave them in for too long or they will become dry.

Serve the quails with tabouleh and some lemon wedges. Pita bread goes well with this.

Red Braised Lamb Shank on
Sweet Potato Mash

100 ml (3½ fl oz) vegetable oil

10 lamb shanks

salt and pepper

flour (for dusting)

300 g (10 oz) carrots, cut into 1 cm (½ in) cubes

300 g (10 oz) onions, cut into 1 cm (½ in) cubes

200 g (6½ oz) celery or celeriac,
cut into 1 cm (½ in) cubes

2 sprigs fresh thyme

2 sprigs fresh rosemary

½ bay leaf

80 g (2½ oz) Sichuan pepper

4 tbsp red wine vinegar

4½ litres (9 pints) lamb jus (see Basics Explained)

1300 ml (2 pints 9½ fl oz) red braising liquid
(see Basics Explained)

10 good quality dried shiitake mushrooms,
soaked overnight

Heat the oil to smoking point. Season the lamb
shanks with salt and pepper and dust with flour,
then sear on all sides until evenly browned. Add the
vegetables to the pan and roast for a few minutes.
Add the herbs and Sichuan pepper then pour in the
red wine vinegar.

When liquid has evaporated add the jus, red braising
liquid and the mushrooms. Cover with a lid or
aluminium foil, braise in a preheated oven at 160°C
(320°F) for about 3 hours or until the meat is well
cooked. Remove shanks and strain the liquid.
If necessary reduce liquid to desired concentration,
add a little butter to sauce if liked.

Serve shanks and sauce on mashed sweet potato or
regular mashed potatoes. Accompany with a selection
of fresh vegetables or cook some root vegetables in
the sauce and serve together.

Another winning dish from the restaurant menu. The amount of red braising liquid used can be varied to suit individual tastes. Sweet potato mash works particularly well in this dish, but regular mashed potatoes can be substituted.

Rendang is a traditional Malay dry beef curry, bursting with flavours of lemon grass, galangal and coconut. It has been a favourite Malay dish since my first visit to Malaysia in 1994. The idea of using rendang spices to marinate raw beef for carpaccio arose when I saw a carpaccio made with beef rolled in lots of herbs. This method of accompanying it with acar and fried shallots is a traditional way of serving rendang as part of a meal.

Rendang-Spiced Beef Carpaccio with Acar

FOR THE RENDANG SPICE MIXTURE

120 g (4 oz) shallots, finely minced

25 g (1 oz) garlic, finely minced

10 cm (4 in) piece ginger, finely minced

50 g (2 oz) medium-hot chilli, finely minced

4 kaffir lime leaves, finely minced

1 tbsp turmeric leaf, finely minced

10 cm (4 in) piece galangal, finely minced

1 stalk lemon grass, finely minced

40 g (1½ oz) freshly grated coconut

75 g (2½ oz) palm sugar

Salt

4 tsp vegetable oil

FOR THE ACAR

2 cups sunflower oil

2 garlic cloves, halved

10 cm (4 in) piece ginger, finely chopped

8 shallots, thinly sliced

1 large medium hot chilli, sliced

5 pieces star anise

1 cinnamon stick

600 g (1 lb 4 oz) carrots, cut into sticks

600 g (1 lb 4 oz) cucumber, cut into sticks

20g (¾ oz) black mustard seeds, crushed

300 g (10 oz) sugar

140 ml (4½ fl oz) rice vinegar

220 g (7 oz) mild red chilli, sliced (red capsicum can be substituted)

220 g (7 oz) mild green chilli, sliced (green capsicum can be substituted)

FOR THE BEEF

1200 g (2 lb 6½ oz) fully trimmed, chilled Australian beef tenderloin

250 g (8 oz) rendang spice mixture

FOR THE GARNISH

Extra virgin olive oil

Parmesan shavings

Crispy fried shallots

Mix together all the ingredients for the rendang spice mixture.

Ensure beef is properly trimmed. Marinate it in the rendang spice mixture for 2-3 hours. Then heat some oil in a large frying pan and sear the beef on all sides. Remove and leave to cool down Spread out some plastic film on top of aluminium foil, roll the plastic film tightly around the beef, and then wrap as tightly as possible in the aluminium foil. Freeze for a day or until needed.

For the acar, heat some of the oil and sauté the garlic, ginger, shallot, hot chilli, cinnamon and star anise until aromas are released. Add carrot and sauté for a further 5 minutes. Remove from the heat and add cucumber, mustard seeds, sugar, vinegar and remaining ingredients. Leave to cool down and marinate for about 6 hours. Keep in the refrigerator until needed. Pineapple pieces or strips can be added before serving.

To serve, put a spoonful of acar, mixed with some gourmet lettuce (frisee, lollo rosso etc.), on a plate, top it with very thin slices of the carpaccio. This is best sliced very thinly using a meat slicer. Top with Parmesan shavings and crispy fried shallots and drizzle some extra virgin olive oil over.

Roasted Veal Cutlets with Wasabi Butter

FOR THE WASABI BUTTER

200 g (6½ oz) unsalted butter

120 g (4 oz) wasabi, use fresh paste

2 anchovy fillets

2 tsp mixed chopped herbs (rosemary, thyme, parsley, chives)

Salt and pepper

FOR THE ROASTED VEAL CUTLETS

4 tsp olive oil

4 Australian free-range veal cutlets

4 sprigs thyme

8 cloves garlic with skin on, crushed

1 sprig rosemary

Make the butter in advance. Soften butter and whip at high speed in a blender to add air; it should have a light and creamy consistency.

Add the wasabi, finely chopped anchovy, herbs and salt and pepper to taste. Whip until all ingredients are well blended. Place butter on greaseproof paper and shape into a roll about 8 cm (3½ in) in diameter. Freeze for at least 12 hours. It can be made a few days in advance and kept in the freezer.

Heat the oil in a frying pan until almost smoking, season the meat well and pan-fry on both sides until well-browned. Add the garlic and herbs to the pan and place in a preheated oven at 230°C (450°F). Roast for about 10 minutes, turn it over once only after 5 minutes.

Place a ½ cm (¼ in) slice of the butter on top of the veal, return to the oven until butter starts to melt, remove and serve immediately.

This method will result in medium to well done veal. The cooking time can be adjusted to suit personal taste. We serve this with mashed potatoes, tomato jam and sautéed spinach.

Wasabi is often called Japanese horseradish. In the West, horseradish is eaten with roast beef, so this dish seemed a good combination. Mixing wasabi with butter works well, it is not overpowering and when melted becomes a sauce.

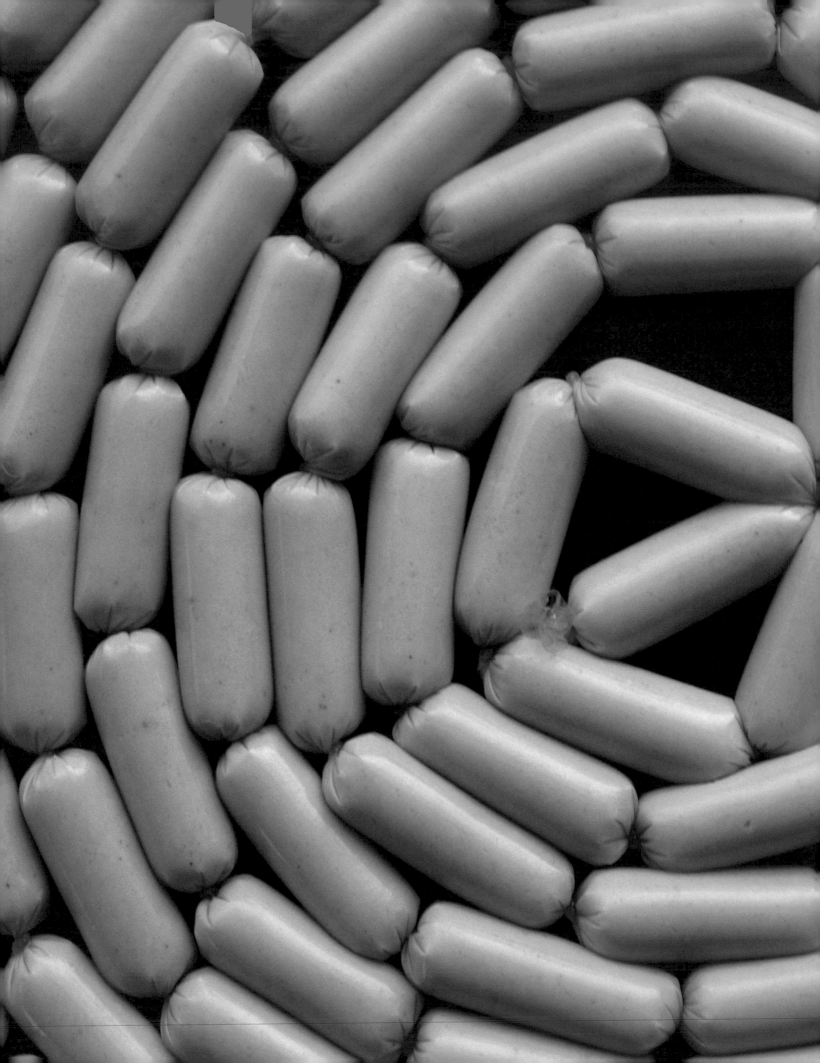

Tandoori Chicken Sausages

2 kg (4 lb) fine chicken sausage meat

2 kg (4 lb) chicken leg meat, chopped

100 g (3½ oz) cheddar cheese, grated

40 g (1½ oz) garlic, minced

2 tsp fenugreek powder

4 tsp red chilli powder

2 tsp cumin powder, made from unroasted seeds

2 tsp cumin powder, made from roasted seeds

2 tsp garam masala powder

30 chilli padi, finely chopped

1 tsp red food colouring

1 tsp yellow food colouring

Salt to taste

Sausage casing

In a bowl, combine all ingredients except the chicken sausage meat and the sausage casing. Leave to marinate for about 2 hours.

Mix in the chicken sausage meat and fill mixture into the sausage casing, making small sausages.

Poach in simmering water until cooked. Do not allow to boil. Remove and either grill immediately or cool down and keep in refrigerator until required.

Serve the sausages with a mint yoghurt dip or mango chutney.

An idea that came about when we wanted to open a delicatessen shop within the hotel a few years ago. Being German, I wanted sausages in the shop, but sausages with a twist.

While working in Thailand, I came to appreciate the wonderful flavours of the local cuisine.
In the northern areas, a popular dish is chicken roasted or 'barbecued' over charcoal fires and served with plain sticky rice.
It tastes a bit sweet and spicy and the charcoal smoke adds another dimension. I adapted the traditional recipe to suit the restaurant.

Thai Roasted Spring Chicken with Mango Salsa

FOR THE MANGO SALSA

100 g (3½ oz) green mango, diced

100 g (3½ oz) ripe mango, diced

100 g (3½ oz) cucumber, peeled and seeds removed, diced

20g (¾ oz) red chilli, cut into fine strips

1 tbsp chopped mint

2 tbsp Thai fish sauce

2 tsp honey

1 tsp white vinegar

FOR THE THAI MARINADE

100 g (3½ oz) red chilli, finely chopped

100 g (3½ oz) chilli padi, finely chopped

100 g (3½ oz) garlic, finely chopped

100 g (3½ oz) shallots, finely chopped

100 g (3½ oz) lemon grass, finely chopped

100 g (3½ oz) ginger, finely chopped

50 g (2 oz) kaffir lime leaves, finely chopped

100 g (3½ oz) coriander leaves, finely chopped

100 g (3½ oz) ginger flower, finely chopped

600 ml (1 pint 3½ oz) vegetable oil

1 tbsp turmeric powder

200 ml (6½ fl oz) Thai fish sauce

200 ml (6½ fl oz) lime juice

FOR THE CHICKEN

2 tbsp vegetable oil

4 spring chickens

400 g (13 oz) Thai marinade

60 g (2 oz) unsalted butter

2 cloves garlic, chopped

160 g (5 oz) baby kailan or choy tam – blanched

80 g (2½ oz) lily bulb

60 g (2 oz) cherry tomatoes, cut into halves

80 g (2½ oz) mango salsa

To make the mango salsa combine all the ingredients and chill.

Combine all the Thai marinade ingredients and mix well. Rub the marinade all over the inside and outside of the chickens.

Heat the oil in a large pan and sear the chickens, sides first. Turn them on their backs so that the breasts are facing upwards. Place in a preheated oven at 200°C (400°F) and roast until done.

In a wok or frying pan, heat the butter and sauté the chopped garlic, then add the choy tam or baby kailan, season with salt and pepper and toss. Add the lily bulb and then the tomatoes. Sauté until all ingredients are hot, check and adjust seasoning.

Serve the vegetables together with the roasted chicken. Pour the mango salsa over the top of the chicken.

Poached Soy Chicken, Asian Mushroom and Soba Noodle Salad

FOR THE CHICKEN

1600 g (3 lb 3½ oz) whole chicken, corn fed free-range if possible

1½ litres (3 pints) water

200 ml (6½ fl oz) light soy sauce, or more depending on your taste

250 ml (8 fl oz) Shao Xing wine or dry sherry

150 g (5 oz) yellow rock sugar (brown sugar can be substituted)

A large piece of ginger, peeled and sliced

3 cloves garlic, sliced

4 pieces star anise

2 sticks cinnamon

3 pieces dried tangerine peel

FOR THE MUSHROOM NOODLE SALAD

4 tsp water

4 tsp palm sugar

4 tbsp tamarind water (see Basics Explained)

2 tbsp light soy sauce

2 tbsp extra virgin olive oil

40 g (1½ oz) unsalted butter

40 g (1½ oz) black wood ear fungus, fresh or reconstituted

40 g (1½ oz) enoki mushrooms, roots cut off

40 g (1½ oz) oyster mushrooms, sliced

40 g (1½ oz) straw mushrooms

40 g (1½ oz) shiitake mushrooms, sliced

Salt and freshly ground black pepper

150 g (5 oz) cooked soba noodles

FOR THE PICKLED CUCUMBER

1 cucumber, hothouse if possible

Sprinkling of sea salt

4 tbsp rice wine vinegar

30 g (1 oz) caster sugar

In a tall slim pot bring all the ingredients for the chicken to the boil, except the chicken. Simmer for 20 minutes, and then add the chicken. Leave to simmer for about 30 minutes over slow heat, cover with a lid and remove from heat. Leave the chicken to cool down in the stock. When cool, remove bones and skin. Keep meat aside until required.

To make the salad dressing, combine water and palm sugar in a pot and cook until it caramelises, then add the tamarind water and soy sauce. Remove from heat and leave to cool. Add the olive oil, stirring it in vigorously. Add two teaspoons of the cooking liquid as well and season to taste.

Heat the butter and sauté all the mushrooms until cooked. Season with black pepper and a little salt.

Peel and slice the cucumber and sprinkle with sea salt, leave for about 30 minutes then wash off the excess salt and pat dry with a kitchen towel. Place in a bowl and add the vinegar and sugar. Leave to cure for about 30 minutes before serving.

Combine the noodles, mushrooms and chicken meat and toss with the dressing. This salad can be served cold, or heat it through gently and serve warm. Top with the pickled cucumber.

Serving suggestions: Top with slices of fresh mango, or sprinkle with a few sesame seeds before serving. Prawns, yabbies or crab meat can be used instead of chicken.

Another of Adam's interesting creations, demonstrating his acceptance and interpretation of new ideas. Poached soy chicken is traditionally Chinese; adding mushrooms and Japanese noodles makes it a truly trans-ethnic dish.

Having worked with many Mexicans and being a lover of the world's breads and sandwiches, I thought it only natural to combine the wonderful texture of a flour tortilla with a crunchy filling full of flavours. It can be served cold, although it is tastier hot.

Chinese Roast Duck Tortillas

6 flour tortillas

FOR THE TORTILLA FILLING

½ Chinese roast duck, de-boned and meat shredded

3 Chinese cabbage leaves, blanched and shredded

30 g (1 oz) snow pea shoots

30 g (1 oz) bean sprouts

2 large red chillies, seeds removed and
thinly sliced

1 tsp roasted peanuts, chopped

½ Asian cucumber, peeled, seeds removed
and cut into thin strips

½ daikon radish, peeled and cut into thin strips

3 tbsp sesame oil

3 tbsp plum sauce

1 tbsp hoi sin sauce

Salt and pepper

FOR THE DIP

6 tbsp light soya sauce

2 chilli padi, finely chopped

2 tbsp peanut oil

Combine all the filling ingredients. Toss well and if
necessary adjust seasoning with salt and pepper.

For the dip, combine all the ingredients and mix well.

Place an equal amount of filling onto each tortilla
and roll into a tight cigar shape. Cut the ends straight
and then once diagonally through the centre.
Arrange standing up and serve with the dip.

Kaffir Lime Leaf-Crusted Lamb Loin with Indian Spiced Eggplant, Goat Cheese Wan Tans and Galangal Gazpacho Sauce

200 ml (6½ fl oz) olive oil

20 kaffir lime leaves

Zest of 1 lime

4 tbsp chopped coriander leaves

4 trimmed Australian chilled lamb loins,
160 g (5 oz) each

4 servings Indian spiced eggplant
(see Vegetables section)

8 tbsp galangal gazpacho sauce
(see Basics Explained)

8 tbsp lamb jus (see Basics Explained)

4 servings goat cheese wan tans,
2 pieces per serving (see Basics Explained)

Heat the olive oil and deep-fry the kaffir lime leaves until crispy. Remove, drain and break into little pieces.

Cool down the olive oil and once cold add the lime zest, coriander leaves and the lime leaf pieces. Add the lamb loins and leave to marinate for at least 6 hours.

Heat some of the oil and pan-fry the lamb loins to desired doneness. Leave to rest in a warm place for about 5 minutes before serving.

Heat the eggplant and sauces, and deep-fry the wan tans. Serve arranged together on a plate or serve all items separately.

It may seem like too many flavours, but the combination works wonderfully well.
This dish has been a popular addition to the menu.

Lemon Grass-Skewered Smoked Chicken Fillets

FOR THE CHICKEN

10 chicken fillets

5 stalks lemon grass, cut in half lengthways and shortened to about 15 cm (6 in).

FOR THE GAZPACHO

300 ml (10 fl oz) cold water

300 g (10 oz) ripe Roma or vine ripened tomatoes, skins removed

1 red capsicum, seeds removed

½ green capsicum, seeds removed

½ medium red onion, chopped

½ cucumber, peeled

1 garlic clove, chopped

2 chilli padi

Juice of 1 lime

Salt and pepper

Chopped coriander leaves, optional

FOR THE MARINADE

1 tbsp honey

1 tbsp balsamic vinegar

1 tbsp vegetable oil

1 kaffir lime leaf, finely chopped

Combine all ingredients for the marinade.

Skewer the chicken fillets with the lemon grass stalks. Marinate the chicken skewers for no longer than 20 minutes before grilling them. Use dry coconut husks to barbecue the chicken – use alone or put some pieces over a regular charcoal fire.

Make the gazpacho not more than two hours before serving. Place all ingredients for the gazpacho into a blender and blend to a smooth consistency, season to taste and keep chilled until ready to use.

Just before serving check again for seasoning and stir well. Add some chopped fresh coriander if liked.

Serve in a shooter glass. Accompany the chicken skewers with lemon or lime wedges and use the gazpacho as a dip.

This is a favourite cold/warm combination. The chicken is charred over a coconut husk fire and the spicy gazpacho complements and balances the sensation.

The cuisine of Korea is not very well known, but it has wonderful food to offer. My favourite, and that of most foreigners visiting or working in the 'land of the morning calm', is barbecued beef ribs, kalbi gooi. I have used this marinade for chicken wings, tenderloin steaks and baby back ribs, and it works with almost anything. This recipe is adapted from the original Korean version, taught to me by Mrs. Kim, the Korean restaurant chef at the Seoul Hilton.

Korean-Style Barbecue Beef Ribs

FOR THE MARINADE

6 tbsp sugar

6 tbsp rice wine or sake

2 tbsp chopped spring onions

2 tbsp ground sesame seed

2 tbsp sesame oil

¾ cup Korean soya sauce (if not available use Chinese dark soya sauce mixed half and half with Japanese soya sauce)

½ cup barbecue sauce, bottled

½ cup chilli sauce, bottled

1 tbsp HP sauce

1 tbsp Worcestershire sauce

Garlic salt

Freshly ground black pepper

Sesame salt, if available

1 kg (2 lb) short beef ribs, cut so that each piece has about 5 bones

Combine all the marinade ingredients and mix well.

Gently simmer the ribs in stock or plain water until the meat is almost cooked. (Traditionally, in Korea, the ribs are not boiled before they are marinated; however, this first partial cooking makes them more tender.)

Remove ribs from cooking liquid and leave to cool down. Place in a suitable container and pour marinade over. Cover and leave to marinate for 12-16 hours.

Remove from marinade and drain, and then grill the ribs over a charcoal grill or barbecue.

A good accompaniment is the Thai green papaya salad, *Som Tam* – the spiciness and crunchiness of the salad complements the sweetness of the ribs.

Grilled Asparagus and Jambugo Ham Bruschetta with Gazpacho Dressing

FOR THE GAZPACHO DRESSING

¼ cup finely diced red capsicum, seeds removed

¼ cup finely diced green capsicum, seeds removed

¼ cup finely diced yellow capsicum, seeds removed

1 small cucumber, peeled, seeds removed and finely diced

1 medium red onion, finely diced

2 tbsp white wine vinegar or lemon juice

200 ml (6½ fl oz) fresh tomato juice

5 tbsp extra virgin olive oil

1 bunch fresh basil leaves

Salt and freshly ground black pepper

FOR THE BRUSCHETTA

4 thick slices ciabatta bread, brushed with extra virgin olive oil and crushed garlic

8 stalks of asparagus, peeled and grilled

160 g (5 oz) jambugo ham

To make the gazpacho dressing, place half of the capsicums, cucumber and onion with the vinegar and tomato juice in a blender. Blend thoroughly and slowly add the olive oil. Season with salt and pepper and keep in the refrigerator for at least two hours.

Combine the rest of the vegetables with the gazpacho dressing and basil leaves. Check seasoning again before serving, it will probably need more.

Marinate the asparagus with a little olive oil and lemon juice.

Grill the ciabatta (which has been brushed with olive oil and garlic) over a charcoal fire, until it is crusty on all sides.

To serve, arrange the asparagus and jambugo ham on top of the ciabatta and spoon the gazpacho dressing over and around.

A typical trans-ethnic dish, marrying Italian and Spanish cuisine. This simple Mediterranean-inspired dish was created by Sid Hardy, Chef de Cuisine at the Fullerton Hotel, for our outdoor seating area by the river. Jambugo, with its bold and robust flavour, good texture, saltiness and lingering taste, is one of the great air-dried hams of the world.

Desserts are a delightful indulgence. They are the ultimate comfort food for many people.

There are few Asian desserts in comparison to the huge range of Western-style puddings and sweets, although a variety of sweet snack foods are eaten throughout the day. At the end of an Asian meal, fruit or sweet soups are generally served.

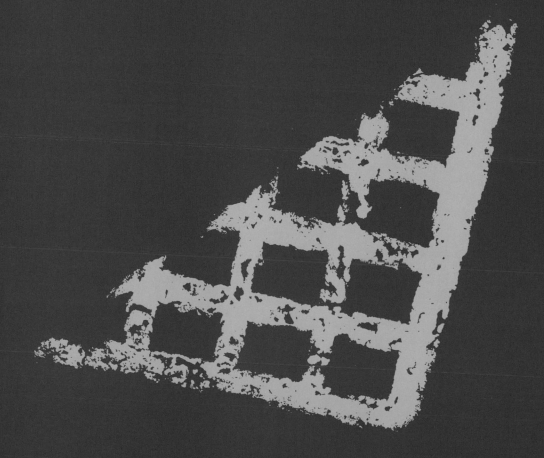

sweets

Green Tea Ice Cream

1600 ml (3 pints 3½ fl oz) fresh milk

75 g (2½ oz) milk powder

170 g (5½ oz) butter

120 g (4 oz) glucose

50 g (2 oz) high quality green tea powder
(the best quality tea makes the best ice cream)

175 g (6 oz) egg yolks

340 g (11 oz) sugar

1 tsp ice cream stabilizer or
2 leaves of gelatine

In a pot, combine the fresh milk, milk powder, butter, glucose and green tea powder and bring to a boil. Remove from heat and leave to cool slightly.

Combine the egg yolks and sugar and whisk well. Stir in the cooled milk and slowly heat up again while stirring continuously, until it reaches 83°C (180°F) – use a cooking thermometer to check this.

Next, add the stabilizer or gelatine and leave the mixture to cool down. Then transfer to an ice cream maker and follow the instructions.

Serve when ready, or store in the freezer at -18°C (0°F). This ice cream should be used the day it is made; after that, it begins to lose flavour.

Whoever first thought of making tea ice cream must be congratulated, as it is a superb flavour.
Green tea is also used to flavour cakes and sauces.

Here is a different view of fusion. This meringue-based confection is the quintessential Australian dessert, adapted from a concept introduced to Australia by Italians. Pavlova is moist and light with a crisp crust, in contrast to the dry European meringues that turn to powder when bitten. Fresh strawberries are used here, but any fruit or fruit compote can be used. If preferred, whipped cream can be used instead of mascarpone cream. This is Jean Paul Bruneteau's version. At the time I worked with him in Thailand he owned Riberries, a leading Australian 'bush tucker' restaurant.

Honey Pavlova with Fresh Strawberries and Lime-Mascarpone Cream

FOR THE PAVLOVA

240 g (8 oz) egg whites

2 tsp white vinegar or lemon juice

480 g (15½ oz) sugar

80 g (3 oz) toasted macadamia nuts, chopped

FOR THE LIME-MASCARPONE CREAM

250 g (8 oz) mascarpone cheese

1½ tbsp honey, leatherwood or similar

Zest of 1 lime

Juice of 1 lime

300ml (10 fl oz) cream, whipped

FOR THE MARINATED STRAWBERRIES

200 g (6½ oz) strawberries, washed and hulled

1 tbsp honey, leatherwood or similar

A few drops of lime juice

When making meringues it is imperative that the mixing bowl is free of grease or any other particles. It is also vital that not even the slightest speck of egg yolk is present, as the fat content of the egg yolk will prevent the egg whites from stiffening. Line a tray with baking paper, use a little water on the underside of the paper to make it stick.

In a stainless steel bowl or in a food processor, whisk the egg whites with the vinegar until they form a soft peak. Gradually add half the sugar to the egg whites, whisking until stiff. Fold in the remaining sugar with a rubber spatula. Place mixture into a piping bag with a large round plain-hole nozzle. Pipe long strips onto the baking paper and sprinkle with the macadamia nuts.

Bake in a preheated oven at 150°C (300°F) for about 20 minutes. Cover with a tea towel and leave to cool. The meringues should be slightly dry on the outside but moist and chewy on the inside. Once they have cooled down, place in an airtight container and use within a few days. If stored for too long they will become dry.

Bring the mascarpone to room temperature and stir in the honey, lime zest and lime juice. Fold in the whipped cream and place in the refrigerator for about 1 hour. Marinate the strawberries with the other ingredients and keep at room temperature until needed. (Room temperature fruit has more flavour than chilled.) Arrange the mascarpone cream on a plate and top with pavlova and strawberries.

Garnish with extra macadamia pieces, and drizzle a little more honey over the top. Serve immediately.

Glutinous Rice Dumplings Filled with Dark Chocolate

350 g (11½ oz) glutinous rice flour

300 ml (10 fl oz) water

75 g (2½ oz) wheat starch

110 g (3½ oz) caster sugar

100 ml (3½ fl oz) boiling water

150 g (5 oz) vegetable shortening

600 g (1 lb 3½ oz) finest quality bitter dark chocolate (min 58% cocoa content)

100 g (3½ oz) walnuts, chopped.

Combine the rice flour and the cold water in a mixing bowl and knead to a soft dough.

In a separate bowl, combine the wheat starch and sugar. Add the boiling water to it and mix to a dough. Then knead in the glutinous rice dough and the shortening. Continue kneading until you achieve a smooth elastic texture. Wrap in plastic film and keep aside for about 2 hours.

After 2 hours, divide the dough into 40 g (1½ oz) pieces. Chop the chocolate into large chunks (about 25 pieces). Roll out the pieces of dough on a rice-floured surface and fill with dark chocolate and walnut pieces. Wrap each dumpling into medallions that are sealed well on all sides; they should look like large scallops. Place on greaseproof paper or banana leaf and steam for about 8 minutes.

After steaming, place in a greased pan or wok and pan-fry both sides of each dumpling over low heat until golden brown. Serve immediately.

Jereme Leung, my very creative Chinese chef, developed this recipe. The combination of softly melting chocolate and chewy rice dumpling casing with the crunchiness of the walnuts is wonderful.

This dish is adapted from an Australian recipe. It makes an enjoyable sweet snack or can be served as a dessert, accompanied by fruit sherbet. Any combination of fruit can be used for the filling.

Sticky Rice and Papaya Steamed in Banana Leaf, with a Honey Syrup

FOR THE SYRUP

200 ml (6½ fl oz) water

100 ml (3½ fl oz) honey, leather-wood or similar

100 g (3½ oz) palm sugar (gula melaka)

FOR THE RICE PARCELS

2 cups Thai glutinous rice

¼ cup water

400 ml (13 fl oz) coconut cream

2 screwpine (pandan) leaves, tied in a knot

¼ cup honey, leatherwood or similar

Pinch of salt

1 piece banana leaf (or cling film)

½ papaya, peeled, seeds removed and cut into small strips

To make the syrup, mix all the ingredients together and bring to a boil, stirring to dissolve sugar. Remove from heat and allow to cool slightly.

Soak the rice in the water for about 1 hour, then drain well. Combine rice, coconut cream and pandan leaves in a pot and bring to a rapid boil. Reduce heat and leave the rice to simmer gently for about 20 minutes, stirring it frequently.

Add the honey and salt and cook for another minute. The rice should be well cooked with a thick, paste-like consistency. Remove from the pot and leave to cool.

Cut the banana leaves into squares of about 20 cm (8 in). Grease the inside lightly. Once the rice is cold, place some rice on the centre of the leaf, top with papaya and top again with rice, make neat little squares so that the papaya is covered completely.

Wrap the banana leaf firmly around the rice, like a parcel. Place parcels seam side down on a perforated tray or dim sum basket and steam for about 10 minutes.

Serve immediately, unwrapped, with syrup on the side or poured over.

This is based on a popular, typically very sweet and heavy, Indian dessert. It is traditionally made with sweet, lightly caramelised syrup; substituting maple syrup adds another dimension to it. Saffron ice cream goes very well with this dessert.

Gulab Jamun with Maple Syrup

300 ml (10 fl oz) Khoya
(see Basics Explained)

50 ml (2 fl oz) Chhenna
(see Basics Explained)

2 drops rosewater

1½ tbsp all-purpose flour

1 pinch bicarbonate of soda

500 ml (1 pint) water

1 litre (2 pints) maple syrup

900 g (1 lb 13 oz) sugar

2 litres (4 pints) corn oil,
for deep-frying

Mix the khoya and chhenna together with the rose-water. Add the flour and bicarbonate of soda. Knead gently until all ingredients are well mixed, but do not over mix.

Roll the dough into even-sized balls (about 26). Heat the oil over medium heat and deep-fry the balls until they are golden brown. Remove and drain on absorbent paper.

Combine the maple syrup and sugar with the water and heat until it starts to simmer. The proportion of water to maple syrup can be adjusted, depending on required sweetness.

Place the balls in a stainless steel container big enough to accommodate them plus the liquid. Pour the syrup over them and leave to stand for at least 1 hour before serving. The longer you leave them, the more syrup the balls will soak up.

Reheat in a microwave oven or on the stove over low heat. This is best served warm with ice cream.

Woo Gok – Deep-Fried Taro Dumplings Filled with Strawberries and Bananas

600 g (1 lb 3½ oz) taro root, peeled

100 g (3½ oz) wheat starch

100 ml (3½ fl oz) boiling water

3 tsp sugar

1 tsp bicarbonate of ammonia

75 g (2½ oz) vegetable shortening

pinch of salt

600 g (1 lb 3½ oz) strawberry-banana compote (see Basics Explained)

2 litres (4 pints) sunflower oil for deep-frying

Cut the taro into large pieces and steam for 20-30 minutes. Make sure the pieces are not small or there will be too much liquid in the dough. Remove from the steamer and leave to dry off briefly. Using a mixer with a paddle, mix well until you have a smooth mash.

Add boiling water to the wheat starch and combine well. Add sugar, bicarbonate of ammonia and the wheat starch paste to the taro and blend into a smooth dough. Add the vegetable shortening last and blend thoroughly.

Remove the dough from mixer, put it in a clean bowl and cover with a tea towel. Place in the refrigerator for at least 2 hours. Then divide the dough into 40 g (1½ oz) pieces, fill each with a spoonful of compote, and shape it into a pointed egg-like form.

Deep-fry the dumplings in a large wok or pot over medium heat, a few at a time, until they are golden brown. Carefully remove and drain.

The crust of each dumpling should be totally made up of crisp little filaments. Serve hot.

Woo gok is a popular deep-fried dim sum with a crust that looks like hairs. Traditionally it is served as a savoury dim sum, reducing the salt content and filling it with fruit makes a wonderful multi-textured dessert. A custard and fruit combination can also be used as a filling.

Hot fruity desserts served with ice cream, this is without doubt the ideal combination.
The abundance of the ingredients in Malaysia inspired this particular dessert.

FOR THE SPICE MIXTURE

6 tsp cinnamon powder

2 tsp nutmeg powder

2 tsp fennel powder

1 tsp ginger powder

FOR THE PINEAPPLE MIXTURE

60 g (2 oz) unsalted butter

1 kg (2 lb) pineapple,
peeled and diced

100 g (3½ oz) caster sugar

1 pinch spice mixture

FOR THE CRUMBLE TOPPING

200 g (6½ oz) butter

200 g (6½ oz) caster sugar

400 g (13 oz) pastry flour, sieved

1 level tbsp dry yeast

To make the spice mixture mix all the spices together and blend thoroughly.

In a large pot melt the butter over medium heat and add the diced pineapple. Sauté for a few minutes without colouring the pineapple. Sprinkle in the sugar and a pinch of the spice mixture and reduce the heat to low. Stir and leave to simmer until the pineapple is soft but not mushy.

Remove and leave to cool. This can be made a few days in advance if necessary.

For the crumble topping, first melt the butter. Mix the sugar, flour and yeast together then pour in the butter and work with your fingers into a crumbly mixture.

Lightly butter the sides of a baking dish, place the pineapple mixture into it and top with the crumble. Bake at 180°C (355°F) for 15 minutes or longer, depending on the depth of the mixture.

Serve hot with ice cream. Coconut ice cream complements the flavours in this dish perfectly.

Pandan Tiramisu

120 g (4 oz) mascarpone cheese

1 tsp pandan extract (see Basics Explained)

50 g (2 oz) sugar

4 tsp water

50 g (2 oz) egg yolks

200 g (6½ oz) cream, whipped

1 tsp green food colouring, optional

8 ladyfinger biscuits (sponge fingers) soaked in pandan syrup (available in bottles)

2 tbsp passion-fruit coulis, sweetened (available frozen)

Place the mascarpone cheese in a stainless steel bowl and leave to soften at room temperature for about 1 hour, and then mix in the pandan extract and green colouring, if used.

Combine the sugar and water and bring to a rapid boil, then remove from heat. Place egg yolks in a mixing bowl, add boiled sugar and water slowly, whisking constantly until you have a foamy consistency: this is called a sabayon. Fold the sabayon into the mascarpone, using a soft spatula. Then fold in the whipped cream.

In a coffee cup or other suitable container, layer the mousse with the soaked ladyfingers. There should be three layers of mascarpone and two layers of ladyfingers. Chill in the refrigerator for at least 4 hours.

Serve garnished with a spoonful of passion-fruit coulis.

This dessert was created especially for a distinguished guest in honour of his son's wedding. His instructions were that it be typically Western, but with a local flavour that his guests could identify. In addition, it had to be green. Roxan, The Fullerton's pastry chef, prepared this interpretation of a classic recipe.

Asian Dried Fruit dipped in Chocolate

100 g (3½ oz) dried pineapple

100 g (3½ oz)) dried mango slices

100 g (3½ oz) dried papaya slices

100 g (3½ oz) dried coconut shavings

100 g (3½ oz) dried Chinese pear

100 g (3½ oz) dried persimmon

100 g (3½ oz) candied ginger

200 g (6½ oz) fresh strawberries

150 g (5 oz) dark chocolate

150 g (5 oz) white chocolate

Melt the dark chocolate and the white chocolate in separate bowls. Take each of the fruit pieces and dip into the melted dark or white chocolate, leaving about half of the fruit exposed.

Let the excess chocolate drip off, then place fruit pieces on greaseproof paper or cling film. Leave to set.

Serve as a snack or after dinner with coffee.

Exotic dried fruits such as papayas, pineapples and mangoes are a popular snack in Asia. A selection of these dried fruits dipped in chocolate makes an unusual and delicious after-dinner presentation to serve with coffee. Add some chocolate-dipped strawberries and the effect will be a multitude of colours.

While designing a new menu a few years ago, the idea of making a sweet spring roll came up. I can't remember who suggested it, but I immediately liked it. Since then we have come up with all sorts of filling to use in a sweet spring roll, from banana-fig combinations to chocolate-walnut and apple-cinnamon. This version is our latest discovery, and a favourite of ours because of the local fruit we use.

Mango and Jackfruit Spring Rolls

400 g (13 oz) jackfruit flesh

2 medium-size mangoes

30 g (1 oz) unsalted butter

60 g (2 oz) sugar

30 g (1 oz) honey, leatherwood
or similar

100 ml (3 ½ fl oz) water

2 tbsp chopped mint

6 - 16 pieces spring roll skin
(depending on amount of filling
used per roll)

2 litres (4 pints) corn oil for
deep-frying

To remove the mango flesh, take a whole mango, cut it into half lengthways, cutting around the big flat seed in the centre. Using a large spoon, almost as large as the mango halves, scoop out the flesh in one piece. With a knife, slice off as much flesh as possible from around the stone.

Chop the jackfruit and three of the mango halves, as well as the cut-offs from the mango stones, into a semi-pulp.

Heat the butter in a pan large enough to accommodate all the ingredients. Sauté the fruit for a minute or two over medium heat and then add the sugar, honey and the water (if fruit is very sweet, reduce or eliminate sugar content). Simmer over slow heat until the mixture is reduced to a thick jam and most of the liquid has evaporated. Remove from heat and leave to cool.

When cold, add the mint and mix well. Lay out the spring roll sheets and fill them with fruit mixture topped with a slice of the leftover mango halves. Roll tightly, first folding in the ends, and seal with a cornstarch and water mixture.

Deep-fry in hot oil until golden brown. Drain on absorbent paper and serve while hot.

Serve with vanilla sauce, chocolate sauce or ice cream. The combination of hot fruit with a crunchy coating and ice cream works particularly well.

NORTH TYNESIDE COLLEGE

LEARNING RESOURCE CENTRE

During my career, I have worked in many different places, and wherever I work, I always hold to certain principles.

The most important is to pay great attention to my raw materials. This starts with respect for the earth itself, so I try to conserve natural resources by using only sustainable products. I spend time with primary producers such as farmers and fishermen to learn about their methods and understand their challenges. In a large hotel, it is not possible to know about every supplier, but I try to obtain detailed information about the sources of certain key ingredients such as meat, fish and seafood.

Before choosing a supplier, chefs must first consider their needs in detail. If we take beef as an example, chefs must decide on the degree of marbling required and then choose either grain-fed or grass-fed cattle. They must then consider what brands are available to them and compare prices. The next step is to learn as much as possible about the producers that seem suitable. One significant point to consider is which abattoirs they use, as small abattoirs usually do a better job than large ones.

Consistent good quality is the single most important reason for choosing a supplier; so regular taste testing is essential. This is especially true if buying from somewhere that does not have clearly defined standards. It is easier to buy from a country such as the USA, which has a long history of national grading standards in beef production or Australia, which is currently putting a very comprehensive grading system into practice.

Chefs should follow the same principles when choosing a lamb supplier. I suggest Welsh blackface or Australian lamb and I would always choose to buy from the nearer country.

My rule with fish and seafood is to buy locally and never import unless absolutely necessary. My reason for this is not price, but freshness. It is much better to use a fresh local fish than import a particular variety that has been dead for many days. The exception is specialty lines such as fresh and smoked salmon. Again, these should be bought from the nearest reliable supplier.

Naturally, every location presents different opportunities and challenges. In Asia, huge amounts of chicken are consumed, but it is difficult to find information about breeders. I base my decisions on the cleanliness of the slaughterhouses, how the processing is done and whether the products are stored and chilled properly. Consistency is again the key. Since Asians are very discerning, we are fortunate here to be able to obtain most of our poultry fresh and not frozen. It is always better, when possible, to buy poultry locally rather than import.

The same applies to fruit and vegetables, although due to the Asian climate, many varieties are not grown here. Herbs, I believe, should always be fresh; dried ones do not have the same flavour.

Few dairy products are manufactured in Asia, but excellent quality products are successfully imported and readily available. I prefer Irish or French butter because of the low water content. Cream is another product about which I am particular. I always choose and recommend natural real cream; never use over-processed products or 'shaving-cream'. As most Asian countries do not allow the import of unpasteurised cheese, many of the major European cheeses are not available here. The proximity of Asia to Australia has helped me to find some very good products there.

When sourcing chocolate for cooking, I always buy the finest quality. Look for products with a high cocoa butter content. Good oriental herbal shops are easy to find here in South-East Asia, but not always in the Western world. Most large Western cities have an area of Asian specialty shops but research and planning are essential to find the right ingredients.

To sum up: my principle is to use fresh, top quality products because they are the key to good food.
Happy cooking.

Rainer Zinngrebe
Singapore, 2001

SUPPLIERS AND SUPPORTERS

BEEF AND LAMB

Over the years, I have tried beef from America, Australia, New Zealand, the UK and Argentina. As all of these countries produce some good and some bad products, deciding which to choose is not easy. Consistency is an important consideration for every chef, along with good quality.

I always used American meat products until about six years ago when I tasted some top quality Australian products. Today I will, if my favourite brand is available, choose the Australian ones, especially in the same price category.

Lamb suppliers I prefer are Hills of Darling, Castricum Brothers (who also produce top quality beef) and Ambassador.

I am so confident about the superior quality of these beef and lamb products that I have asked Meat and Livestock Australia (MLA) to support this book. I trust that Tim Kelf and others at MLA will continue to increase awareness of their products the world over, and that the producers will support not only these efforts, but also the recently implemented Meat Standards Australia 'eating quality assurance' programme.

FISH AND SEAFOOD

Aquatas from Tasmania has been my favourite supplier for many years, not only of fresh salmon but also superb salmon roe and an excellent range of smoked salmon products. I invited the company to be part of this book, as I believe they are leaders in salmon production and processing. Anton Dacomo, a Swiss national, leads the Aquatas team.

In Europe, I would use Scottish or Norwegian salmon.

CHEESE

One of the biggest Australian manufactures is Lactos from Tasmania; they produce top quality 'delicatessen' cheeses under the Cradle Mountain label. When ripe and served at the correct temperature, these cheeses rival the best on offer from France. Red Square is one variety worth a special mention.

Of course, there are other good Australian cheeses. The best I have found are Heidi Farm Cheese, Timboon Farmhouse Cheese and Tarago River Cheese Company. The selection is huge, and again the main decisive factor besides quality is consistency.

This section explains the basics required for most of the recipes. These are things such as stocks, spice mixes and sauces. You will find details of where these basic components come from, what they are normally used for and suggestions about where else they can be used. They are intended to stimulate a cook's imagination and not only to be used for the recipes in this book.

basics explained

All conversions shown are approximate, see abbreviations and conversions section for more details.

You will notice there are no serving quantities given. The number of servings depends on whether the dishes are served Asian style or Western style. In a typical Asian meal several dishes are offered, and diners are served or help themselves to a little of everything. The recipe quantities will serve fewer people if served Western style in main course portions.

The limes used in these recipes are the local *limau nipis* – a juicy thin-skinned lime about the size of a lemon.

Chilli padi is the local name for tiny, fiery red or green chillies. *'Padi'* means rice, true *chilli padi* are almost as small as a grain of rice. Today the name is also used for bird or bird's-eye chillies – it has come to mean any very small, very hot chilli. Use with caution.

Shao Xing (or Hsing) is used in several recipes. This is a Chinese cooking wine; if it is not available dry sherry can be substituted.

Capsicums are also known as bell peppers.

ASIAN-STYLE CHICKEN STOCK – MAKES 1 LITRE (2 PINTS)
This is an excellent basic stock, which can be adapted to suit any purpose. Khun Sawakit, my assistant, taught me this during our time in Bangkok. I prefer this stock to the normal Chinese chicken stock as by adding onion, garlic and coriander root you get a broader and fuller flavour.

2 kg (4 lb) chicken (boiling hen), preferably free range with a high fat content

300 g (10 oz) onions, quartered

3 spring onions

1 bunch coriander leaves or small bunch coriander roots

3 cloves garlic, crushed

20 cm (8 in) piece ginger, sliced

5 litres (10 pints) water

Chop the chicken into 5cm (2 in) pieces, combine all the ingredients in a pot large enough to leave a 10cm (4 in) space to the rim. Bring to a simmer. Leave to simmer until chicken falls off the bone, remove from heat, take out chicken and strain. Reduce the stock to about one litre or to the concentration you require. This excellent basic stock can be enhanced with pork ribs to make what the Chinese call a 'supreme stock'. From this stock you can make soups, sauces or even jellies.

BÈCHAMEL SAUCE
This basic sauce is an essential part of many dishes such as lasagne and cannelloni. This recipe will make about 1 litre.

60 g (2 oz) butter

80 g (3 oz) flour, sieved

1 litre (2 pints) milk

A pinch of grated nutmeg

1/8 bay leaf

1 clove

1/4 onion (clove stuck through bay leaf and into onion)

1/8 tsp salt

Heat a pot that will hold all the ingredients comfortably. Over medium heat melt the butter, once it starts to bubble stir in the flour.

Cook for a few minutes. Remove from heat and allow to cool down.

Heat the milk and gradually add it to the flour and butter (roux), stirring, constantly. Add nutmeg and the onion with the bay leaf and clove. Bring to a simmer over medium heat and then reduce heat to low.

Simmer for 30 minutes. Add some more milk if necessary. Adjust seasoning and strain through a fine strainer or cheesecloth.

CLEANING BIRD'S NEST
Soak bird's nest in cold water for 6 hours, ensuring it is totally submerged. Drain and wash to remove any feathers or other debris. Then totally submerge in hot water for 24 hours. Change the hot water three times during this period. Drain well, press all the water out and reserve until needed.

COOKING PULSES
When cooking pulses certain rules must be followed. First place the required amount into a pot or bowl and place under cold running water. Once the bowl starts to overflow stir the pulses with your hand a few times, this is to bring to the surface any unwanted particles. Leave under gently running water until the water runs clear. Before cooking, most pulses should then be soaked overnight in room temperature water at a ratio of 1 part pulse to 3 parts of water.

Cooking is best done in a container large enough to accommodate the pulses plus the water plus the same volume again, as some pulses can expand almost out of the pot.

When boiling pulses use the same water ratio: 1 part pulses to 3 parts water. Use fresh water for boiling the pulses unless you are planning to make a black bean soup, when you use all the soaking water as well.

Put the pulses into a pot with the water and bring to a rapid boil. Leave the pot uncovered and do not season the pulses with anything as this will cause them to 'harden' and cooking will take much longer. This also applies to soups made from pulses, only season them after they are cooked.

Leave to boil until they are cooked, then strain and spread them out on a large flat surface to cool down. I do not like 'shocking' them with water as it causes them to loose a lot of their natural taste.

CRAB MEAT WAN TAN
I remember during my first visit to Hong Kong, watching a traditional wan tan maker beating the skins flat with a bamboo pole. These Chinese wan tan skins are very versatile. They can be filled with any choice of ingredients and then formed into ravioli or the more familiar shapes such as moneybags. They can be deep-fried or boiled.

12 pieces wan tan skin, 10 cm (4 in) square

120 g (4 oz) crab meat

1 tbsp mayonnaise

1 tsp chopped medium-spicy red chilli

1 tsp chopped spring onion

1 tsp chopped shallots

Salt and pepper

Combine the crab meat, mayonnaise, chilli, spring onions, shallots and season with salt and pepper.

Place equal amounts in the centre of each wan tan skin. Wet the edges of the skin with water and fold over into a triangle. Press the edges together tightly to seal.

Cook in boiling water or deep-fry in hot oil for about 2 minutes. Drain well and serve.

DUCK SAUCE
I often use leftover Chinese roast duck pieces for this, because they give the sauce extra depth.

1¾ kg (3½ lb) duck bones, wings and carcasses (no fat)

1 large onion, chopped

85 g (3 oz) carrots, chopped

115 g (4 oz) leeks, chopped

2 tomatoes, cut into chunks

2 cloves garlic

2 tsp sunflower oil

100 ml (3½ fl oz) red wine

1800 ml (3 pints 10 fl oz) Asian chicken stock

600 ml (1 pint 3½ fl oz) veal stock

½ bay leaf

1 sprig thyme

20 black peppercorns, crushed

1 tbsp unsalted butter

Heat the oil in a roasting pan to smoking point. Add the duck bones and place the roasting pan in a preheated oven at 230°C (450°F). Leave them to roast until they are evenly browned, and then add all the vegetables to the pan. Roast until the vegetables are brown and start to caramelise, as this will release their natural sweetness, but make sure they do not burn.

Transfer the bones to a pot and deglaze the roasting pan with red wine, scraping up the caramelised bits. Pour this over the bones and add the stock. Bring to the boil and skim from time to time. Once the stock has been simmering for about an hour and not much more scum is coming to the surface, add the herbs and peppercorns. Leave to simmer for a further 2 hours and then strain through a muslin cloth.

Return to a clean pot and reduce to required strength. Just before serving season the sauce and finish by stirring in some cold unsalted butter.

DUCK STOCK (MAKES 1 LITRE) This is similar to chicken stock, but with an added depth of flavour.

4 kg (8 lb) leftover Chinese roast duck carcass and/or roasted duck bones

300 g (10 oz) onions, quartered

3 spring onions

1 bunch coriander leaves or small bunch coriander roots

3 cloves garlic, crushed

20 cm (8 in) piece ginger root, sliced

5 litres (10 pints) water

Chop the duck into 5 cm (2 in) pieces, combine all the ingredients in a pot large enough to leave a 10 cm (4 in) space to the rim. Bring to a simmer. Leave to simmer for 1½ to 2 hours, remove from heat and strain.

Reduce the stock to about 1 litre (2 pints) or until it is the strength you require. This is a useful stock to have on hand, it can be enhanced with pork ribs to give it more body.

FISH STOCK I learned the basics of fine cookery from Pierre Koffmann, and today I still use his recipes or variations. This is one of them.

1 litre (2 pints) cold water

500 g (1 lb) white fish bones, chopped into large pieces

50 g (1¾ oz) unsalted butter

1 carrot, sliced

1 large onion, sliced

1 stalk celery

1 large leek, white part only, sliced

200 ml (6½ fl oz) dry white wine

4 sprigs parsley

½ bay leaf

2 sprigs thyme

20 white peppercorns, crushed

Sauté the vegetables in the butter over low to medium heat until they are soft but not coloured.

Add the fish bones, sauté for another minute then add the wine. Cook slowly for about 5 minutes. Add water and bring a boil, then skim the surface, reduce the heat and add parsley, bay leaf, thyme and peppercorns.

Simmer gently for about 20 minutes, and then strain the stock through a fine sieve or muslin cloth.

FRESH MANGO CHUTNEY A great accompaniment to many dishes, this version is far superior to the sweet types available in supermarkets. My friend and colleague Bag Singh Negi who worked with me in Thailand and Malaysia created this recipe for a special event function. We enjoyed it so much we served it as a spread for bread.

1 medium red onion (sweet Maui onion is ideal), finely diced

2 fresh garlic cloves, finely chopped

50 g (1¾ oz) good quality unsalted butter

2 tbsp rice vinegar or white wine vinegar

500 g (1 lb) ripe mango, diced. Use mangoes that are not too sweet e.g. Thai elephant mango

100 g (3¼ oz) medium-ripe mango (to add chunky texture), diced

500 ml (1 pint) water

120 g (4 oz) caster sugar

¼ tsp mustard seeds

1 pinch rock salt

In a pot that can accommodate all the ingredients, melt the butter over medium heat and add the onions. Sauté until onions are transparent then add the garlic. Sauté for about 2 minutes stirring constantly.

Add the mango, sugar, vinegar, mustard seed and water and bring to a simmer. Stir constantly with a wooden spoon over medium heat for about 30 minutes, or until it reaches the consistency of a thick puree or pulp.

Season to taste with salt. Leave to cool. This can be kept in the refrigerator for a couple of days, but it is best used within a week.

GALANGAL GAZPACHO SAUCE This is a great sauce for lamb, chicken or fish. We use it typically as one of two sauces on a plate. When two sauces are used for a dish, the contrast in flavours intensifies the effect of individual ingredients.

2 tsp extra virgin olive oil

1 small onion, finely chopped

large piece of galangal, peeled and thinly sliced

6 cloves garlic, minced

3 red capsicums, roasted, skin and seeds removed

4 chilli padi, seeds and stems removed

2 tsp tomato paste

1 tsp paprika powder

3 tsp red wine vinegar

440 ml (14 oz) tinned plum or Roma tomatoes

1 small cucumber, peeled and finely diced

Salt and pepper

Heat the oil over moderate heat and sauté the onions, galangal and garlic until onions are transparent.

Add the chilli padi and capsicum and sauté for a few minutes. Add the tomato paste and paprika and cook for another 3 minutes or so.

Add the vinegar and cook until reduced by half, and then add the tomatoes and the cucumber. Boil for about a minute, remove from heat and blend to a pulp. Strain and bring back to the boil. Reduce if necessary to desired thickness.

Adjust seasoning with salt and pepper. To make it spicier, add some Tabasco.

GOAT CHEESE WAN TAN Wan tan skins can be used to wrap almost anything and then either deep-fried or boiled. When boiled they become almost transparent. I like using them because they are never doughy. They are very difficult to make and I recommend buying them ready-made.

1 large potato, boiled and mashed (use a floury variety, not waxy)

60 g (2 oz) goat's cheese (more if you want a stronger flavour)

2 tsp chopped coriander leaves

2 tsp extra virgin olive oil

8 - 16 wan tan wrappers, depending on filling used per wan tan

2 litres (4 pints) vegetable oil for deep-frying

Combine the potato, goat's cheese, coriander leaves and olive oil and mix well. Place little mounds of filling on to the wan tan skin and fold over like ravioli. Wet the edges with a little water and squeeze together to seal. Deep-fry in hot oil until golden brown and crispy and serve immediately.

HARISSA CRUST An idea borrowed in principle from Moroccan cookery, harissa is essentially a spice mixture. We make a paste from it which is used to coat lamb, chicken or other items. It adds an extra dimension to simple foods, but it must be used carefully since it can overpower the entire dish.

200 g (6½ oz) dried chilli flakes

14 cloves garlic, finely minced

4 tbsp coriander seed, roasted and ground

4 tbsp cumin seed, roasted and ground

4 tbsp caraway seed, roasted and ground

2 tbsp extra virgin olive oil

400 g (13 oz) mint jelly

100 g (3½ oz) freeze dried breadcrumbs (Japanese, if possible)

½ bunch mint, chopped

½ bunch coriander leaves, chopped

Zest of 4 lemons

Combine all the ingredients and keep refrigerated until needed.

INDIAN SPICE MIXTURE (FOR PAN-FRYING)
This mixture was invented for my Indian Spiced Seabass, but it can be used as a spice seasoning for lamb or any other items I use this in many dishes because it is distinctive yet not overpowering.

1 part cumin seed

1 part fennel seed

1 part coriander seed

1 part ajwain seed

In a dry frying pan, roast all the seeds over medium heat until they start to crackle. Remove and pound to a coarse powder with a pestle and mortar.

JAPANESE SALAD DRESSING
This is Adam's version of a Japanese-style salad dressing without sesame oil. Instead of the traditional turnip, it uses apple for additional fruitiness.

1 green apple

3 cloves garlic

3 shallots

250 ml (8 fl oz) rice vinegar

600 ml (1 pint 3½ oz) salad oil

2 tbsp black Shoyu soy sauce

4 tsp English mustard powder

Salt and freshly ground black pepper

Using a fine grater, grate the apple, garlic and shallots. Combine all the ingredients together and mix well. Season to taste with the salt and pepper. Leave for at least 2 hours for the flavours to infuse before using it. This dressing should be made fresh daily, as the grated shallots will spoil it quickly.

JUS
The principle here is the same whether you are making lamb, veal or any other jus. The objective is a clear, brown reduction of flavours that should never be bitter. Basic recipe for Lamb Jus – makes about 1 litre (2 pints)

4 tbsp vegetable oil

1800 g (3 lb 10 oz) lamb bones, chopped into small pieces

1 large onion, diced

1 large carrot, diced

¼ piece celeriac or 1 stalk celery, diced

1 glass red wine

4 cloves garlic

1 sprig thyme

2½ litres (5 pints) iced water

In a 220°C (430°F) hot oven, heat a large enough roasting pan to accommodate all the ingredients. Add the cooking oil and once it starts smoking add the bones.

Leave to roast until the bones are golden brown, turning them occasionally. Once they are golden brown, add the vegetables and roast again until the vegetables start to caramelise. Remove tray from the oven and drain off the fat, returning the bones and vegetables to the tray. Place back into the oven and after 2 or 3 minutes deglaze with the red wine.

Remove all ingredients from the tray and transfer to a pot. Add the iced water, garlic and thyme and bring very slowly over slow to medium heat to a simmer.

During the cooking process, skim the surface frequently. Leave to simmer for about 2 hours and then drain through a fine strainer or muslin cloth. Return to a clean pot and reduce over medium heat until you have about 1 litre of jus remaining.

KHOYA AND CHHENNA
Indians have various types of cheese-like dairy products. These two are used for making Gulab Jamun, a well-known Indian dessert.

Khoya
2 litres (4 pints) fresh milk, full fat

Chhenna
2 litres (4 pints) fresh milk, full fat
160 ml (5 fl oz) white vinegar (or rice vinegar)

For the Khoya, place milk into a Teflon coated wok or pan (unless you have what the Indians call a kadhai). Bring milk to the boil and reduce heat to low. Stir occasionally, and simmer gently until milk is reduced by half.

From then on stir constantly and at the same time scrape down the layer of dried milk that will form on the sides of the wok or pan. Reduce further until you obtain a product of mashed potato consistency. The amount left at the end is about 400 g (13 oz); it will take between 1¼ hours and 1½ hours to make this product. Place in a stainless steel bowl and refrigerate. It will last for up to 48 hours but not much longer.

For the Chhenna, place milk into a pot and bring to the boil. Remove from heat and leave to cool to 48°C (120°F). Pour vinegar in a steady stream over the entire surface and stir until the milk curdles (this will take about 3 minutes). Pour the curdled milk into a strainer lined with muslin cloth. Leave for a while for the whey (clear excess liquid) to drain off.

Now pick up the muslin and squeeze until the clear whey changes to a very milky whey. What remains is something that resebles cottage cheese, this is called Chhenna. Place it on a tray and while still warm, knead it with the palm of your hand until all granules have gone. Place in a refrigerator for up to 24 hours.

LAKSA PASTE
You can make your own or purchase a ready-made product from an Asian supermarket.

This recipe will make about 500 gram (1 lb) of paste, which you can freeze in batches.

250 g (8 oz) shallots, finely chopped

100 g (3½ oz) garlic, finely chopped

80 g (2½ oz) ginger, finely chopped

80 g (2½ oz) galangal, finely chopped

100 g (3½ oz) lemon grass, finely chopped

150 g (5 oz) dried shrimps, finely chopped

100 g (3½ oz) medium size red chillies (chilli boh)

10 chilli padi

1 cup vegetable oil

30 g (1 oz) fresh curry leaf, chopped

40 g (1½ oz) turmeric powder

80 g (2½ oz) fish curry powder (a ready-made curry powder available in Asian supermarkets)

Combine the shallots, garlic, ginger, galangal, lemon grass, dried shrimp and chilli in a blender. Add half of the oil and blend to a smooth paste. Heat the remaining vegetable oil to medium heat in a pot or wok large enough to accommodate all the ingredients.

Add the blended mixture and fry slowly, stirring it constantly for about 5 minutes or until you have a very fragrant aroma coming from the pot. Now add the curry leaf, turmeric powder and curry powder and fry for another 2 minutes. Leave to cool down and use when needed.

LEMON GRASS WATER
Cooking with lemon grass can make a dish slightly bitter in taste. Using lemon grass water will prevent this happening.

1 litre (2 pints) water
20 stalks fresh lemon grass, crushed

Put lemon grass into cold water and slowly bring to a simmer, do not boil as this will release the unwanted bitter taste. Simmer for 20 to 30 minutes, remove from heat and leave to infuse for a further 2 hours until the water is cool. Strain and store in refrigerator.

MAYONNAISE
Chefs have argued about whether you should buy mayonnaise ready made or make your own – my opinion is it depends on where you are in the world, what you use it for, what climatic conditions you have and how many staff you have available.

Certain recipes call for homemade mayonnaise because you can vary the flavour. Here is a basic mayonnaise recipe to which any flavour can be added.

8 egg yolks

2 tsp white wine vinegar

3 tsp Dijon mustard

1700 ml (3 pints 6½ fl oz) salad oil, sunflower or similar

About 2 tbsp lemon juice

Salt

Make sure all ingredients are at room temperature. Place egg yolks in a stainless steel bowl. Add the mustard and vinegar to the yolks and mix well. Stir in the oil drop by drop so it can emulsify. Once all the oil is absorbed, adjust to desired tartness with lemon juice and season with salt.

PANDAN JUICE OR EXTRACT Pandan is the leaf of the screwpine tree and it is used throughout South-East Asia as a flavouring or colouring agent. It is also used to wrap foods that are then baked in the leaves.

This extract is very easy to make, but the squeezing must be done gently or the bitterness of the pandan oil will come through.

30 g (1 oz) pandan leaf, finely chopped

250 ml (8 fl oz) cold water

Place pandan leaf and water into a blender and blend until you have a very green juice. Strain through a muslin cloth and squeeze lightly. Keep in refrigerator until needed.

RED BRAISING LIQUID Adam developed this version of Jereme's recipe for a fragrant and sweet sauce. It can be used to braise anything from oxtails to lamb shanks and, of course, in Asia it is traditional with pork knuckles.

20 cloves garlic, fried whole

20 g (¾ oz) star anise

15 g (½ oz) cinnamon stick

15 g (½ oz) dried ginger

2 pieces old ginger

110 g (3½ oz) fermented red bean curd

150 g (5 oz) brown bean paste

4 tbsp oyster sauce

4 tbsp dark soya sauce

2 tbsp sugar

150 ml (5 fl oz) Shao Xing wine or dry sherry

3 litres (6 pints) Asian chicken stock

A few drops sesame oil

1 tbsp chicken stock powder, or one stock cube

Combine all the ingredients and cook for about 20 minutes over moderate heat, leave to infuse for at least 6 hours then strain the liquid. Keep aside in the refrigerator until needed.

RISOTTO A good risotto is not easy to make, it needs undivided attention for about 20 minutes and cannot be rushed.

Two things define a good risotto. First is the rice, which must be an Italian risotto rice (Arborio,

Carnaroli, Roma, Riso Baldo and Vialo Nano are some of the better known varieties).

Second is the cooking process:
Melt unsalted butter in a saucepan large enough to hold all the ingredients and more. Add chopped onions and fry slowly over low to medium heat until these become transparent. Add the rice (not rinsed) and sauté over slow heat until the rice toasts nicely and becomes slightly translucent. Make sure you do not use too high a heat as this will burn the butter.

Now stock is added to the rice a ladleful at a time. The heat should be such that the stock is not quite boiling. Add more stock when needed and after about 15 minutes check and taste if the rice is cooked. It should be al dente and this normally takes anywhere from 15 to 20 minutes, depending on the rice and the heat.

The consistency is very important. It should not be too soupy but at the same time not dry and lumpy. It should have a creamy, moist texture with every grain separate yet all holding together, almost like a thick sauce. Add some more pieces of butter and stir in grated Parmesan cheese.

Season it with salt if necessary. The Parmesan cheese alone is sometimes sufficient. Freshly ground black pepper should be added to taste and then it should be served immediately with more Parmesan cheese on the side.

Basic risotto ingredients for 4 servings:

80 g (3 oz) onion, finely chopped

1½ litres (3 pints) stock (fish, chicken or vegetable)

100 g (3½ oz) unsalted butter

60 g (2 oz) grated Parmesan cheese

approx. 150 g (5 oz) risotto rice (resulting volume varies depending on variety used)

STRAWBERRY-BANANA COMPOTE
2 tbsp Demerara sugar
1 vanilla bean, split
1 banana, diced
10 strawberries, diced
1 tbsp Grand Marnier
10 macadamia nuts, coarsely chopped

Melt the sugar in a pan big enough to accommodate all the ingredients. Add the vanilla bean and then the strawberries and banana. Cover and leave to simmer over a slow heat for about 5 minutes.

Remove cover and add Grand Marnier and macadamia nuts. Drain off excess juice into another saucepan, and over medium heat reduce the juice to a syrup.

Pour the syrup back over the fruit and leave to cool down, chill in the refrigerator before using.

SUN-DRIED TOMATO SAMBAL This sambal is not spicy and goes wonderfully well with all sorts of fish or meat dishes.

2 tbsp extra virgin olive oil

1 tbsp chopped dried shrimps

2 tsp dried chilli flakes

½ medium-hot red chilli, finely chopped

2 cloves garlic, finely chopped

6 shallots, finely chopped

100 g (3½ oz) sun-dried tomatoes (not the dark extra dry variety, home made ones that have some moisture left are best), finely chopped

1 tbsp tomato paste

Juice of 4 small limes

30 g (1 oz) palm sugar

Heat the olive oil over moderate heat and add the shrimps, chilli, garlic and shallots. Sauté until the shallots are transparent then add the sun-dried tomatoes. Sauté for about 5 minutes, and then add the tomato paste, lime juice and sugar. Cook slowly for a further 5 - 10 minutes. Leave to cool and keep until needed.

SUSHI RICE There are several suitable types of rice available. I prefer to use Koshikari or Nishiki rice, but an American Calrose can be used.

250 g (8 oz) sushi rice

330 ml (11 fl oz) water

40 ml (1½ fl oz) sushi su

Wash the rice and soak it for 30 minutes in water. Drain well and transfer to a rice cooker. Add the water and cook for about 45 minutes or until the rice cooker indicates it is ready.

Transfer the rice into a wooden or stainless steel bowl. Wait until it has cooled down to about 40°C (105°F), then add the sushi su and mix it in well with the rice. Cover and use as needed.

SUSHI SU This is the basic mixture required to prepare sushi rice, you can also turn this into an interesting salad dressing by adding some lemon juice and a little sunflower oil.

720 ml (1 pint 7 fl oz) Japanese sushi vinegar (Mitsukan Shiragaru)

660 g (1 lb 5 oz) sugar

160 g (5 oz) salt

5 g (¼ oz) dry konbu (Japanese Seaweed)

Mix the ingredients together and warm in a pot to about 45°C (110°F), just warm enough to dissolve the sugar. Do not boil the mixture as this will destroy the taste of the vinegar.

TAMARIND WATER Used in much of South-East Asian cooking, tamarind has a wonderfully acid taste that lifts the flavours of many dishes.

2½ litres (5 pints) water
1 kg (2 lbs) fresh tamarind pulp

Combine the two ingredients and mix well until the tamarind is almost totally dissolved. Strain and use the water.

THAI RED CURRY PASTE This is our version.

10 large red chillies

2 tsp coriander seeds

1 large piece galangal, peeled and chopped

1 stalk lemon grass, finely chopped

4 cloves garlic, minced

1 shallot, chopped

1 tsp lime juice

2 tsp groundnut oil

5 kaffir lime leaves

Place all the ingredients in a blender and mix to a thick paste. Vary the quantities of each ingredient according to your personal taste. If the paste is too oily, leave it to sit for about 30 minutes at room temperature and skim off some of the oil.

Keep either in a refrigerator or in small batches in the freezer.

TOMATO-HERB MIXTURE I add this mixture to a variety of dishes that do not need sauces, it is very 'Italian' but also very neutral so it can be added to almost any dish or eaten on good bread.

I prefer Italian or South Australian olive oils; use Colonna or any high quality extra virgin olive oil for this recipe.

100 g (3½ oz) ripe Roma tomatoes, skinned, seeds removed and cut into ½ cm (¼ in) cubes

1 small red onion, finely chopped

1 tbsp chopped Italian (sweet) basil leaf

1 tbsp chopped Thai basil leaf

1 tbsp dill, shredded by hand

400 ml (13 fl oz) extra virgin olive oil

Pinch freshly ground black pepper

Pinch sea salt

Combine all the ingredients and keep at room temperature until needed. It should be made a few hours in advance so the flavours can infuse. This is best eaten at room temperature, as the flavours are far more robust.

TOMATO JAM Since visiting Australia, I have come to love using jams and chutneys with my food. This is Adam's recipe, which is easy and very tasty. We serve it with meats and sometimes on its own with freshly baked bread.

250 g (8 oz) caster sugar

125 ml (4 fl oz) dry white wine

2 tbsp white wine vinegar

2 large onions, cut into 1 cm (½ in) cubes

600 g (1 lb 3½ oz) whole very ripe tomatoes, (vine ripened if possible) cut into large chunks

½ bay leaf

Reduce sugar, wine and vinegar to a syrup, then add the onions and simmer for 15 minutes. Add bay leaf and tomatoes and simmer for about an hour or longer depending the consistency you want. Season if necessary with salt and pepper.

VEAL OR LAMB STOCK Although these stocks are different, the recipes are very similar. For lamb stock, perhaps add more thyme and rosemary and some garlic cloves, but the method remains the same. The ice is used to bind small unwanted particles and bring them to the surface for easy removal.

1½ kg (3 lb) veal bones or lamb bones, chopped to a large walnut size

3 tbsp tomato puree

2 large carrots, chopped

2 large onions, chopped

1 celeriac, chopped

3 tbsp chopped mushrooms, or mushroom trimmings

2 medium size tomatoes, chopped

500 ml (1 pint) red wine

1 kg (2 lb) ice cubes

3 litres (6 pints) cold water

1 sprig thyme

1 sprig rosemary

⅓ bay leaf

Brown the bones in a roasting tray in a preheated oven at 230°C (450°F), turning them from time to time. Once they are nicely browned spread the tomato puree over them and continue roasting for another 10 minutes or so.

Remove the bones from the roasting pan and place in a pot. Add the vegetables to the roasting pan and return to the oven. Roast the vegetables until they are brown but not burnt. Add them to the pot with the bones. Deglaze the roasting pan with the red wine and pour the juices onto the bones.

Add the ice and the water and bring slowly to a simmer, skim frequently for about an hour, then add the herbs and simmer for about 6 - 8 hours. Strain the stock through a muslin cloth and reduce to required strength.

VEGETABLE STOCK A great base stock for vegetarians. There are also good vegetarian stock powders available in supermarkets.

2 tbsp vegetable oil

2 large onions, chopped

1 clove garlic, crushed

2 large carrots, chopped

1 leek, white part only, chopped

1 celery stalk, chopped

5 button mushrooms, halved

2 tomatoes, chopped

⅛ bay leaf

3 litres (6 pints) water

In a pot large enough to hold all the ingredients, heat the oil over medium heat. Add the onions and garlic and sauté until the onion is transparent. Add the carrots, leek, celery and sauté for another 2 minutes. Then add all the other ingredients.

Turn the heat to high and once the stock starts to boil, reduce to a simmer. Leave to simmer for about 45 minutes. Strain through a fine sieve and bring back to the boil. Leave to reduce until about 1 litre (2 pints) of stock is left. Store this stock in the refrigerator or freeze it in small batches.

XO SAUCE This sauce has nothing to do with cognac. This version is pork-free, as are all recipes in this book.

150 g (5 oz) soaked Chinese dry scallops, about 50 g (2 oz) dry product

Peanut oil, sufficient to just cover all the ingredients

150 g (5 oz) garlic, chopped

150 g (5 oz) shallots, chopped

150 g (5 oz) dried shrimps

75 g (2¾ oz) medium-hot red chilli

75 g (2¾ oz) red chilli padi

30 g (1 oz) dried chilli

30 g (1 oz) roasted shrimp paste (belacan)

1 tbsp dried shrimp roe

150 g (5 oz) chicken stock powder

30 g (1 oz) sugar

Tear the soaked dried scallops into shreds. Heat some of the oil and shallow fry the scallops until they become very crispy, remove and drain.

Be very careful during the deep-frying process, as the scallops splatter a lot. Over medium heat bring the rest of the oil up to frying temperature and add the garlic, shallots and dried shrimps. Fry on low to medium heat, stirring constantly, until these ingredients are nicely browned.

Add all three types of chilli; fry for a few seconds, then add the belacan and finally the scallop shreds. Cook for about 2 minutes together until all the ingredients are well infused.

Remove from heat and leave to cool down. Add the seasonings and stir well. Pour into a bowl and keep in a cool dry place – not the refrigerator – until needed. It should keep for about a month.

acknowledgements

First, I must thank Shekar for asking me to make this book with him. Without his photography, I would never have known where to start. I also want to express my appreciation to Peng, Shekar's wife. As a Chinese married to an Indian vegetarian, her natural approach to fusion has been a great inspiration to me. Shekar and Peng share a passion for food, and Peng's knowledge and understanding of classic Asian cuisine styles has inspired some great 'Chinese-Indian' fusion dishes.

Thank you to Joe Lam and Wei Ming of Chimera Design for putting together our ideas so wonderfully. Frederick Lim for helping out with some of the food styling.

Ms Farah Khan supported this book by kindly allowing us to use crockery and artefacts from her store.

A big thank you to all the cooks who helped along the way, especially Jereme Leung, Eugene Shio, Bag Singh Negi, Thierry Marais, Jeff Leheude, Richard Long, Anthony Dawson, Sid Hardy, Roxan Villareal, Jeffrey Siew and Louis Tay. Those I have left out – thank you, I remember you all.

I would also like to thank Tim Kelf, Tim Bower and Russell Patterson for their ongoing support and their commitment to promoting and producing such great ingredients – which help to make me look good.

I am grateful for the encouragement of Martin Schnieder and Wolfgang Krueger during all my projects. Also thanks to MPS Puri and Ivan Lee for making this venture possible.

Finally yet most importantly, I want to thank all the professionals who helped me with dedication, inspiration and support for this project – especially Adam. He was the executor of the ideas while I was caught up with the day-to-day business of running a big hotel kitchen.

THE TEAM

RAINER ZINNGREBE Rainer Zinngrebe began his working life in 1980 as an apprentice chef at a local hotel in Dortmund, Germany. After national service in the air force, he joined Inter-Continental Hotels in Frankfurt. In 1985 he was transferred to the May Fair Inter-Continental London and then moved on to Pierre Koffmann's La Tante Claire. From London he returned to Germany's Duesseldorf Hilton. After two years there, Rainer was transferred to the Drake Hotel in Chicago.

From the United States he moved to Asia, first as a chef for Margaux, a French fine-dining restaurant at the Kowloon Shangri La, then to Korea as Executive Sous Chef at the Seoul Hilton. He was transferred again as Executive Sous Chef to the KL Hilton, his first Malaysian posting. From there he went as Opening Executive Chef to the Sheraton Grande Sukhumvit in Bangkok, returning to Malaysia for the opening of the Mandarin Oriental Kuala Lumpur.

Rainer has been Executive Chef at The Fullerton Singapore since its opening. Some of the recipes in this book can be found on the menus of its outstanding food outlets. These include sophisticated bistro and brasserie restaurants, a Cantonese

fine-dining restaurant, avant-garde bars, alfresco and fine-dining restaurants and banqueting facilities catering for up to a thousand people.

ADAM ROZMARYNIEWICZ Born in Tasmania, Adam started his cooking career at the age of sixteen. He completed a three-year indentured apprenticeship at Drysdale House Hospitality College, where he also worked in a small restaurant. After finishing his apprenticeship, he moved to mainland Australia and worked in several different cities at five-star hotels and freestanding premiere restaurants.

Adam then travelled to Europe, working and studying for two and a half years in hotels. Mainly working in the German, French and Italian regions of Switzerland, he absorbed the European culture and work ethic. Back in Australia he worked again in major cities for five-star properties and independent restaurants. This led to 'guest chef' cooking promotions in Asia with Melbourne restaurateur Bill Marchetti of Marchetti's Latin, which in turn led to Adam's decision to continue cooking in Asia.

He was involved with the opening in Kuala Lumpur of the Mandarin Oriental, where he worked closely with Executive Chef, Rainer Zinngrebe. He credits Rainer with giving him a wider understanding of Asian culture and cuisine. As Adam says, "His guidance has given me insight and he has become a close friend whom I deeply respect. I believe that cooking must first be a passion and I am sure that the best chefs are those who remain true to the basics".

Until recently Adam was Chef de Cuisine Pacifica at the Mandarin Oriental Kuala Lumpur. He has now joined the Kempinski Hotel Beijing Lufthansa Center as Executive Sous Chef.

SC SHEKAR Educated in Kuala Lumpur and Australia, Shekar began as a photojournalist at the STAR newspaper in the early 80s where his work won the Malaysia Press Photo Awards in 1983 and 1986. In 1989, he became an independent photographer specialising in editorial, architecture, hotels and resorts, and food photography.

Shekar's work has appeared in several exhibitions including Movements, KL Arts Festival (1985), Kuala Selangor, A Documentation, National Art Gallery (1989), In Memory of Ismail Zain, National Art Gallery (1992), Documentasi Malaysia, National Art Gallery (1994), Photography As An Art, National Art Gallery (1996) and Vision, A Multicultural Exploration of Malaysia and Austalia, National Art Gallery (1997). His food photography can be seen in the Malaysian Celebrity Cookbook (1993), Hey Good Cooking Series of cookbooks and The Cuzhinhia Cristang Cookbook (1997) as well as numerous other works for many prestigious international hotels and food manufacturers in the Asia-Pacific region. Shekar is regularly commissioned for documentary assignments in India, Sri Lanka, Korea and Papua New Guinea.

Shekar is married to Peng who is an accomplished cook and food stylist responsible for some of the recipes in this book. They have two children Siddharth and Zhen-Zhu. Together, they run Reds Studios in Malaysia.

index